The Boy Captives

Being the True Story of the
Experiences and Hardships of

Clinton L. Smith and Jeff D. Smith

Among the Comanche and Apache Indians
During the Early Days - The Only Two
Brothers Ever Known to Endure the Same
Hardships of Captivity and Get Back Alive.

A Thrilling Tale of Savage Indian Life and
Captivity Truthfully Told by the
Captives Themselves

Tragedies of the Borderland and Perils
of the Frontier Depicted

Written by
J. MARVIN HUNTER

DISTRIBUTED BY
CLINT & NETTIE SMITH
140 RAFTER O RANCH ROAD
JUNCTION, TEXAS 76849
325/446-2086 - 800/523-4277

First Printing 1927
Second Printing 1965
Third Printing 1986
Fourth Printing 1987
Fifth Printing 1993
Sixth Printing 1994
Seventh Printing 1995
Eighth Printing 1996
Ninth Printing 1997
Tenth Printing 1997
Eleventh Printing 1998
Twelfth Printing 1998
Thirteenth Printing 1999
Fourteenth Printing 2000
Fifteenth Printing 2001
Sixteenth Printing 2002

Printed by
San Saba Printing & Office Supply
1609 West Wallace • San Saba, Texas 76877
915/372-3825

ISBN 0-94369-24-9

THE BOY CAPTIVES

Can Still Use the Bow and Arrow

THE BOY CAPTIVES

INTRODUCTORY

In chronicling the experiences of Clinton Lafayette Smith, before, during and after his captivity by the Indians, I do not hesitate to say that after examination of the record which has been furnished me, not only by the subject of this sketch himself, but by others who knew him as a boy and have known him since his return from captivity, that the reader will find in the following pages a true and correct recital of this man's thrilling life story, and which will be of absorbing interest to the reader and the student, and which I consider a splendid contribution to history—an inestimable legacy and gift to posterity, as rare and timely as truth is mighty and eternal.

Clinton L. Smith is now an old man. His life has been one of unceasing hardship; with his hands he has had to toil, and still has to toil, for the necessities of life. He has resided on the frontier of Texas all of his life, and when he was just a small boy, before he was made captive by a band of savage Indians, he was as all other children of the frontier, deprived of schooling and that instruction which is so necessary to develop the young mind and train it for high ideals. Then came captivity for a period of almost five years, and at a time when the youthful

THE BOY CAPTIVES

mind is so receptive for training for good citizenship, character and morality, and he was thrown among savages, to imbibe and absorb the most vicious ideas and develop the most cruel and bloodthirsty nature of the wild men.

Notwithstanding these things, and though he became a savage, and as vicious as any of his adopted tribe, the regeneration of Clinton Smith was accomplished within a few short years after his return to civilization, and he became a good and highly esteemed citizen, and is today known throughout South and West Texas as an upright, law-abiding, honest man.

In telling the story of his captivity he brings to the fore many hitherto un-revealed facts in regard to habits and customs of the Indians. For instance, many writers refer to the Comanches as having maintained permanent headquarters somewhere in the wilds of the uninhabited regions. Clinton Smith says they had no permanent place of adobe, but were "on the move" all of the time, and he tells of the roamings of the tribe while he was with them. He cannot with certainty, name the states or the regions which they traversed, as he has never studied the geography of our country, but he knows their ramblings carried them into the Rocky Mountains, and even to the Pacific coast, across deserts, and into snow-clad

THE BOY CAPTIVES

mountain fastnesses. He became a warrior, and a brave one. He participated in the various ceremonies of the tribe; he learned to ride as only an Indian can ride, and to this good day, despite his advanced age, he can mount and conquer any bronco on the range. As stated above, being at an impressionable age when he was captured by the Indians, he had much intimate contact with the Indian life, motives, habits, superstitions, joys and sorrows, and in his story he reveals glimpses that are interesting and instructive. He says he found much worthy of admiration in the Indian character, in their tribal laws, and domestic life, and having become thoroughly familiar with the Indian viewpoint he found much to praise and defend that in the imagination of white people has had universal and popular condemnation. During his captivity there were cemented between him and many of the Indians ties of strongest attachment; ties which could not easily be severed, and even when the time of liberation from his captivity came, he did not want to leave his red brothers.

Upon his return from captivity Mr. Smith was quick to readopt and experience a complete revival of the inherent sentiments and amenities of civilized life, and some years later he married a splendid and estimable woman, who has been his greatest comfort

THE BOY CAPTIVES

in presiding over his home and sharing with him the blessings of the family they have raised.

In compiling this interesting story we adhere as strictly as possible to the manner of expression, the style of recital and the method of description used by Mr. Smith. To change it to any great extent, we believe, would detract from the main purpose, that of conveying to the reader the true insight into conditions as they rarely existed at that day and time. If we succeed in accomplishing this we will feel that our task has been well performed. Interwoven throughout the narrative of Clinton L. Smith is the story of his younger brother, Jefferson Davis Smith, who was taken captive at the same time, and who also spent several years with the Indians. This lad was sold into the Apache tribe later, and the two boys were thus separated for months at a time. Jeff Smith now lives in San Antonio, Texas, while the elder brother, Clinton L. Smith, lives at Hackberry, Texas.

This book would not be complete without Jeff Smith's story, so it is given, in the proper place by Clinton L. Smith.

J. MARVIN HUNTER

THE BOY CAPTIVES

THE BOY CAPTIVES

PRECEDING any story of our lives, and before entering upon a recital of the experiences we had during the captivity of myself and my brother, Jeff D. Smith, I want to say that my life has been molded in rude elements, without any of the refining influences which an education gives. This story, therefore, has none of the characteristics of a novel in which the imagination supplies every need and meets every emergency. It is my aim to state simple facts, and nothing but the plain truths, as they occurred to me, for I have neither the gift, nor the inclination, to fabricate a story of thrilling adventure just to please the tastes of those who look to the novelist to meet their demand for entertainment.

There are living today a great host of grey haired comrades and acquaintances, whose friendship I esteem beyond every consideration of gain, to who I offer this book. They were pioneers on the frontier, and are now foremost men in their respective communities, and to them I cheerfully refer to the reader for verification of the truthfulness of my utterances. I could not do this if it were fiction, for those sterling gentlemen would not give their endorsement to nor countenance an imposter. Of course I do not presume to say that any set of men can verify the truth of every

THE BOY CAPTIVES

incident here related, but that intrepid host of West Texas pioneers, who were the wards of life and liberty, and are yet the upholders of the country's integrity, had such an intimate knowledge of and association with the affairs of this commonwealths building, that they can say with certainty whether or not the essential elements of this story are true or exaggerated. Among these old frontiersmen was Captain Charles Schreiner, of Kerrville, Texas, recently deceased, who was in command of a body of Minute Men at the time of our captivity, and there are many others who live in various parts of the state who well remember when the Indians came in on a raid and carried us away.

But before relating the story of the capture of my brother, Jeff D. Smith, and myself by the Comanche Indians, which occurred in the winter of 1871, and the subsequent events in our rugged lives, I think it would be proper to tell of some of the incidents of our home life, and how my brothers and sisters and I had escaped capture before that eventful day.

My father, H.M. Smith was born in Pennsylvania. At an early age he was left an orphan, and came with some emigrants to Texas, and settled at Austin. He helped in the erection of the first buildings in that place. My mother's maiden name was Fannie Short. She came from Alabama to Texas when but a girl, and

THE BOY CAPTIVES

she and my father were married at Austin in 1841. They lived near Austin for awhile, but the Indians became so troublesome there they moved to San Antonio, where my father and a man named Jacob Linn established a blacksmith and gun shop, their location being near where the present City Hall stands. Later father became City Marshal of San Antonio, and served in that capacity for quite awhile. In 1861, when the war between the states broke out, he joined the Texas Rangers to serve in the protection of West Texas from depredations by Indians and outlaws. While serving with the Rangers he had many perilous adventures, but being a man who never talked much, he never boasted of the things which he did. After the War he freighted from Indianola, later called Powder Horn, to San Antonio, using two teams of oxen, eight yokes to each wagon. My brother, Willie Smith, drove one team and father the other. When returning from these trips, he would hobble his oxen out near where now stands the City Hall, in San Antonio, and they would graze the streets of the town and wander only a short distance away.

Finally he moved out to Dripping Springs, on the Cibolo river, twenty-seven miles from San Antonio, where he traded a rifle for 640 acres of land, on which there was a little board hut, and it was on this place that most of our family was raised. In those days land was cheap, and not considered very valuable. I have been told that the land which father traded for there cannot now be bought for $60 per acre. We lived on deer, turkey, beef, bear, honey, and corn pone. We had flour bread about Christmas time. As we raised our own corn we grated it on a hand grater and made cornbread. Most of the time we had coffee, but if our supply gave out Mother would roast okra seed and grind it to make coffee.

Game was plentiful, and father would take his gun and go only a short distance from the house and kill a deer for supper, carrying it on his shoulder.

Mother had a spinning wheel and loom and made cloth to supply our clothing needs. Sister Caroline would card the rolls and spin the thread, while Mother would weave the cloth. For coloring and dye they used walnut for black, and various barks and plants to give variety of colors as desired. I have dropped off to sleep many a night listening to the hum and buzz of the old spinning wheel.

Father would tan his own leather made from cowhide, and make shoes for all of us, using pegs made from sumach wood as a substitute for tacks.

In this way we lived, not only we, but all of the other ranchers in that sparsely settled region.

We were a large family, but never had a doctor in our home for sixteen years. It seems now that a family

THE BOY CAPTIVES

cannot do without a physician for one year.

We had a few horses, and about 100 head of cattle. Later Father added sheep to our line of ranching. At that time Brother Jeff was the youngest of our family, he being seven years old. As our stock of sheep increased Father would take his muttons to San Antonio to market, but the demand for them was very limited, eight or ten per day would meet the requirements of the butchers. We would therefore have to herd them about town for several days before we could dispose of one hundred head. This herding fell to the lot of Brother Jeff and myself. At night we would pen the sheep in the back yard of Mrs. Ditler's beer joint, located where North Flores Street crosses San Pedro Creek, and which is now called Five Points. There was no other house there at the time, but a Mr. Cotulla had a beer joint, dance hall and park at San Pedro Springs, a short distance above. I remember quite well that Mr. Cotulla had a hole dug in the ground in which he kept a coyote, a coon, a wild cat and two black bear, and in a large cage he had various kinds of birds. There was not more than seven or eight houses between there and town, at that time. Later John Fest put up a store there, and I understand the establishment is still in operation. I knew every merchant in San Antonio in those days. Among them I knew T.C. Frost when he was selling calico over the counter. That was fifty-

THE BOY CAPTIVES

eight years ago. Now Mr. Frost's bank is one of the largest in that city.

After several days, when Father had sold out our muttons, we would yoke up the oxen, old Sam and Brindy, throw our camp equipment into the wagon and pull out for home, making the trip, a distance of twenty-seven miles, in two days. Now the trip can be made in a Ford automobile in less than an hour.

While my parents were living on Cherry Creek, near Austin, just a few months after their marriage, they were awakened one night by the sound of horses' feet, which Father thought were his horses which he had staked. He started to go to them, but found the house surrounded by Indians. He secured his gun, while Mother got the cap and ball pistol, and opened fire on the Indians, who would dodge about so lively that they were unable to kill one of them. Soon their bullets gave out, and Mother started a little fire in the fireplace and began molding bullets as fast as she could, while Father kept the Indians driven back. In her haste Mother threw some freshly molded bullets out on the floor, and Father poured some powder in his gun, grabbed a bullet, still hot, and rammed it into the gun, and the load was discharged, the bullet going up through the top of the house. Father, in telling us children about the fight, said Mother never got the least bit excited during the fight. The moon was shining

THE BOY CAPTIVES

brightly, and Father finally killed a horse from under the chief, and the Indians left, taking Father's horses with them.

On another occasion, in 1858, Father and some other men were encamped on Catalie Prairie, near Dripping Springs, cutting hay for the Government. One morning at daylight, while they were cooking breakfast, at a water hole on the Cibolo river, a band of Indians attacked them. They put up a desperate fight and killed seven Indians. Three of their party were killed and two were wounded, a man named Peoper, another named Obst, Lish Sheppard, Serol Krauser, and a Mexican named Antonio Arovio.

At another time, when Father was cutting hay with an old fashioned scythe, an Indian slipped up within a few feet of him and suddenly rose up. Father's gun was left standing against a tree nearby, but was out of reach at that moment, so he raised the scythe to cut the Indian in two, but the Indian jumped straight up, putting up both of his hands, and said, "Me Tonk!" Father did not make the stroke, but backed off to where his gun was standing against the tree. The Indian was dressed like a chief, and was well armed. He deliberately turned and walked away. Father was afraid to kill him, for he did not know how many more Indians were hid in the high grass. So he said to himself: "That Indian could have taken my life before I saw

THE BOY CAPTIVES

him, for I did not know there was anyone within a mile of me. He spared my life and I am glad I did the same for him." He must have crawled like a snake through the grass to get there. No one ever knew his reason for the act.

I heard Father tell of a bear hunt he once took, in company with Mr. Staffle who kept the first post office in Boerne, and Mr. Dietert, who owned the first corn mill in that town, and also Mr. Aue, who owned the first store and kept the first post office at Leon Springs, and Mr. W.D. Parrish, who built the first house where the main government camp is today, about five miles east from Leon Springs. I have not been there since 1875 but I can remember every big tree, hill and creek there, for I knew all of them. The party went over on the Balcones, up near the Jack Mountains, and found lots of bear sign, where they had been pulling down limbs to get acorns. They had with them eight of Uncle Tom Short's dogs. It was drizzling rain from the northeast, and they had not gone far before the dogs opened up on a trail which led towards Boerne. They followed and the dogs bayed the bear under a bluff, within five miles of Boerne. Mr. Parrish got the first shot and killed the bear. He was a big one. So they dressed the bear, and each man got a piece and started for home. Father and Mr. Parrish were about twelve miles from home and as they emerged from a deep creek

THE BOY CAPTIVES

they looked back and saw nine Indians trailing them. They watched the Indians until they went down into the deep creek, and they succeeded in getting away from there and reached home safely.

Father was engaged in many desperate fights in the early days. I remember hearing him tell of one fight, while he was on duty with the Texas Rangers in 1839. He said they had a big company of minute men and were camped on some river, the name of which I have forgotten. He said he and twenty-four men were out scouting, about six miles from camp, when they saw an Indian. As they started toward him the Indian ran, and was soon joined by three more Indians. They kept right after the fleeing Indians, and ran into a trap set for them. As they topped a little ridge they discovered about 100 Indians quietly awaiting their approach. Captain Bird, who was in charge of the scout, gave orders to retreat and try to get away. At that moment the Indians gave a yell and dashed toward them. They fought those Indians in a running fight for two or three miles, when they came to a deep canyon, and the Indians succeeded in surrounding them. Captain Bird gave orders not to surrender, but to fight until the last man dropped. It was then about 2 o'clock in the afternoon. The Indians with overwhelming numbers, made repeated assaults, in which the rangers lost all of their horses. The arrows and bullets

THE BOY CAPTIVES

were falling like hail, and the men were forced to seek refuge under rocks and boulders, where they vigorously returned the fire, which was so effective that the Indians were killed in large numbers. The Indians were forced to retire for a time, but they came back repeatedly, and it began to look as if they would succeed in exterminating the Rangers. Just before sundown, a well-directed shot killed the chief, and the fight ended. There were only eight out of twenty-five of the rangers left. Captain Bird was killed. The surviving eight men were without horses, or other means with which to remove their dead and wounded, and were compelled to leave them on the battle field. They set off on foot, and reached camp about 9 o'clock that night. At once the company was made ready to go for the dead and wounded, but they arrived on the battle ground too late, for the Indians had returned there and killed all of the wounded men and had cut their arms off and hung them up in trees. They had scalped some of them, and had removed their own dead and wounded. The next day the Texans tried to overtake the band of Indians, but they got away.

In the early sixties Mexican outlaws were very troublesome, and often robbed ranches for money, and the blame was placed on the Indians. About that time the Bickel family was robbed and killed, only one member of the family, a boy about 12 years old,

THE BOY CAPTIVES

escaping. He ran off and hid in a field while the murderous work was being done. I think this survivor of that tragedy still lives at Boerne. About this time a band of the outlaws conspired to rob and kill our family. These robbers were secreted over on the Helotes, about fifteen miles from our home, and it was known to them that my father had sold his wool in San Antonio, and they supposed he had the money from its sale at his ranch. There was a miscarriage in their plans, however, for all Mexicans were not outlaws, but some were good citizens, and we had a good many friends among the latter class. These murderous conspirators confided the secret of their plot to a Mexican named Juan Lazarene, and solicited his help in the execution of their plans. He did not protest, but seemingly agreed to assist them, but said he would have to go to San Antonio before he could do so. When he had taken his leave he did not go to San Antonio, but came hastily to our ranch to bring us warning of the villainous conspiracy. He reached our place about sundown and informed us of our danger. There were seven of us at the ranch, my two sisters, Amanda and Polly, two of my brothers, Dock and Jeff, and two boys about twelve years old, Bluford, an orphan, Fritz Garvis, and myself. We had only two horses at the ranch at the time, but things began to pick up. The boys got the guns, and five of us rode the two horses,

THE BOY CAPTIVES

while two of us walked. We started for the Martin ranch that night. It began pouring down rain soon after we started, and in a very short time all of the little creeks were rolling down. It was so dark we could only see by the lightning flashes, and we could proceed only with the greatest difficulty. Blueford, who was in the lead with a big gun on his shoulder, boasted of what he could do, but he stepped in a hole of water, fell down, and lost his gun, and we had to search for quite awhile before we found it. We reached the Martin ranch about 2 o'clock in the morning, as wet as drowned rats, and remained there two days. When we returned home we found the Mexicans had been there and had broken open the doors and ransacked the house. We had a narrow escape, I think. Father was gone from home at the time. About twenty men organized and went over on Rocky, found where the Mexicans camped, captured nine of them and hung them to one tree. That stopped the robbing for awhile.

The Tonkaway Indians would sometimes come to our house and on occasions, when they learned there were no men at home, they would order something to eat. They were supposed to be friendly and partly civilized, though there was nothing in their general appearance by which one might distinguish them from the hostile tribes, except by their saying, "Me Tonk". One day Mother and sister saw a band of Indians

THE BOY CAPTIVES

approaching our house, and they immediately secured guns and halted the band before they reached the door. They said, "Me Tonkaway; want to eat." Mother told them to stack their guns against a tree and she would cook something for them. They did so, and Mother soon had food cooking, while my sisters stood guard with guns in their hands. When the meal was prepared Mother placed it on the table and allowed them to come in and eat. They did not manifest any knowledge of the use for which knives and forks were intended, but proceeded to pick up everything with their fingers, and when they had finished eating they began to chatter and laugh. They then pulled off their buckskin jackets and proceeded to gather up all of the food that remained on the table and put it in their jackets, tied them up and walked out. That was but an incident of our pioneer life, for often my mother and sisters stood guard all night when my father was absent from home, while I, in childish fear, would lay with my head covered up, thinking that the Indians would come and kill us all. My Mother and sisters were brave and fearless, and could shoot guns like men. Sister Caroline could ride a horse and rope a cow as quickly as any man, and Father always called her his cowboy.

There were nine children in our family, five girls and four boys, of whom two girls and four boys are

THE BOY CAPTIVES

yet living. They were: Martha, Caroline, Will, Amanda, Jacob Linn (Dock), Polly, Clinton, and Jeff and Lee, twins. Martha married W.P. Graves. She died at her home twenty-five miles north of San Antonio, in 1875. Caroline married Leonard Coker, and now lives in San Antonio. Amanda married Sam Lane, and lives at Bandera, Texas. Jacob Linn (Dock), lives in San Antonio. Polly married Jack Cravey, and died at Boerne, Texas, in 1916. Clinton lives at Hackberry, Texas. Jeff now lives in San Antonio. Lee married Ben Cravey; she died at the old Smith home at Dripping Springs, in Comal county, Texas, in 1893. Father died in 1882. Mother died when I was about six years old.

DODGING CAPTURE BY THE INDIANS

The Indians made five unsuccessful attempts to capture one or more of us children. The first time they tried to capture us, Sister Polly, Brother Jeff and I were at the cow pen near the house, milking one night, when we heard a low whistle. We thought it might be Indians, but we outran them and got into the house. The cattle smelled them and began to run, too. They could easily have killed us, but I am sure it was their intention to capture us.

THE BOY CAPTIVES

At another time I was herding sheep up near the old Green Camp water hole, about two miles from home. I was down in a creek, when I heard horses' feet coming in my direction. I knew that they would have to come down that creek, for there was no other way they could go. Of course I did not know whether the riders were Indians or cowmen, but I did not wish to take any chances, so into a thicket and under a big rock I went like a rabbit. I crawled back as far as I could and then turned around to peep out. They came on down the creek, watered their horses, and then passed on down near me. I could only see the legs of the horses, as they were passing, and could not tell if they were Indians, but I was satisfied they were, and there were about fifty of them. When they were gone and everything was quiet, I came crawling out, bunched my sheep and went home. I did not say anything to the folks about it for fear it might have been cowmen, and that I would be laughed at for being afraid. Later it was proved that they were Indians, for they went over on Curry's Creek, where they killed a man or two and stole a lot of horses. Father heard of them next day.

The third time I escaped capture I was herding sheep and I saw a bunch of Indians a long ways off, and they had discovered my flock of sheep, for they were coming in my direction. Indians had been killing

THE BOY CAPTIVES

Mexican herders in that section, and perhaps thought this flock was in charge of a Mexican. In that locality there were large trees covered with long moss, so up a tree I went, crawled out on a limb, and wrapped up in the moss. The Indians came on a gallop, rounded up my sheep, and rode all around, looking for the shepherd, but they never found me. Some of them came so close to the tree that I held my breath for fear they would look into the tree. Failing to find me they went on. Their faces were hideously painted and they all had long black hair. When they had gone I came down from my hiding place, left the sheep and went home and told Father what had happened. He went after the sheep. We had twelve horses at that time, and several of them came home that evening, "Old Sam," our stallion, had several arrows sticking in his neck, and he died that night. When the Indians could not catch a horse they would try to kill him. After they left me that day they met a Negro belonging to Mr. Parrish and killed him. There were about twenty-five Indians in the band.

The next escape I had was when Brother Dock and I had gone out to look for cows and calves one day. We were riding Father's two buggy horses, "Tobe" and "Clay." They were splendid animals, and I will never forget them. One was a grey, and the other

THE BOY CAPTIVES

was a clay or cream color with black mane and tail. We had to cross the Cibolo to go over south where the cattle ranged. It had rained the night before and the Cibolo was up, about to our horses' knees, and the ground was very soft. When we had ridden about two miles we came up on a little ridge and looked over and saw about seventy-five Indians, who discovered us at about the same instant. We halted, and I told Dock to pull his pistol, but he said it would do no good, and that we would have to outride them and get away. They started toward us, yelling like a pack of blood hounds. Dock admonished me to not whip my horse, but to pull a tight rein, and away we flew. The Indians began to crowd us closely until we came to a hog-wallow flat, about a mile wide, where there were many depressions in the ground which were full of water, and which made running very difficult. Our horses were corn-fed, while those of the Indians were grass fed, and that gave us some advantage, as our horses out-winded theirs as they passed over the soft, boggy ground. We had made a slight gain on the Indians by the time we reached the Cibilo, but to our surprise and dismay, we found the stream bank full from the rain which had fallen above the night before. Dock jerked off our bridles, and with a piece of rope on our horses' necks, into the raging water he went, telling me to follow him, but he came up all

THE BOY CAPTIVES

CLINTON AND JEFF SMITH
In Indian Garb

THE BOY CAPTIVES

right. My horse followed, as if he had been trained to the task, with me clinging on for dear life. Sometimes I would almost lose my hold on the saddle-horn, as the waves would almost go over me, and the drifts would go rushing by. When we landed on the other side, about two hundred yards down stream, we heard the Indians yelling. They had reached the river, but did not seem to dare to venture into the raging stream. We were too far away from them to shoot us, so we arrived at home safely.

The reader will bear in mind that we were just two small boys, and I have often thought of the good judgement used by my brother on this occasion to outwit and outrun those Indians. Just picture to yourself the exciting chase, the howling band of Indians in pursuit, and the quick decision of a frontier lad when he found himself confronted with the choice of captivity by savages or swimming a swollen stream. He wisely chose the latter course.

The fifth time I escaped capture, was when I went out with Uncle Tom Short on one occasion to help him train two hound pups for deer dogs. We were going along in the switch cedars, when we suddenly came upon seven or eight Indians. They saw us at the same time. We turned and ran through the cedars, and after proceeding a short distance, I dodged off and left Uncle Tom. He soon missed me and was

THE BOY CAPTIVES

afraid the Indians would kill me, but the brush was so dense they could not find me. Uncle Tom ran for dear life, with both pups following after him and barking at every step, and the Indians after the pups. The pups made it easy for the Indians to follow him, and the only thing that saved him was when he reached the river he crossed over, and lost the pups. I turned back and reached home before he did. We were both afoot. Uncle Tom said he did not want to train any more dogs afoot.

The sixth time I saw the Indians they caught me, with my brother, Jeff, an account of which is given in the succeeding pages of this book.

THE CAPTURE

It was on the morning of February 26, 1871, when my brother, Jeff Smith, and I went out to herd sheep, while Father went to look for his horses. We had not gone far before we spied something crawling on the ground on a hillside. It looked like hogs or black sheep, and we were puzzled to know just what they were. We stood watching them, and they disappeared, one at a time, over the hill. As Indians had tried to

THE BOY CAPTIVES

catch us before, we sensed something of danger at the strange actions of these suspicious looking objects, so we started back towards home. I knew there was a cave between us and home, and I told Jeff we would go on closer to the cave, and if those things we had seen were Indians we would run into the cave and be safe.

They were really Indians, who were spying around for horses when they saw us, and made up their minds to take us along with them, so they told me afterwards.

While Jeff and I were talking about the cave, we heard the sound of horses' feet approaching, and looking around, we saw the Indians trying to cut us off from our home. We saw their long black hair flying, their red painted faces, their spears and their big shields, and the wild war whoops they gave lent speed to our feet as we bounded away. I held Jeff by the hand, and for a short distance he kept up with me, but the little fellow soon began to tire, and I took him on my back and ran down hill toward the cave, but the Indians closed in upon us about four hundred yards from where we started. One big Indian jerked Jeff from off my back, and then I tried to get away. By

THE BOY CAPTIVES

this time the whole bunch had gotten there, and as I started to run for the cave again, they surrounded me. I ran under one of their horse's belly, but they headed me off, and then I dodged under another horse's neck, but they halted me with guns and tomahawks, so I stopped and looked the big chief in the eye. He spoke to me in a language that I did not then understand, and patted me on the back, so I understood that he meant for me to mount behind him. I walked straight up to him, he took me by the hand, put out his foot for me to get upon, and I did so.

As we road up out of the creek I could see my sisters coming with guns as fast as they could run, but the Indians only laughed at them, for there were twenty-five Indians, ten Lipans and fifteen Comanches. My two sisters and stepmother witnessed the whole scene. It was a sad farewell to all at home as we rode away. While I was looking back I could see my sisters and hear them screaming for Father's help, but he was too far away. In a short time we were out of sight, gone, it seemed, forever.

Father soon returned, and at once thought of trying to head the Indians off from going north. He first went to Boerne, and from there a runner was sent to Fort Concho, 190 miles northwest, where about four thousand soldiers were stationed. They also sent a runner to inform my cousin, Captain John

THE BOY CAPTIVES

W. Sansom, who was at Camp Verde, in Kerr county. He and his men, with blood hounds, came and took the trail, and Captain Charles Schreiner also joined the chase with about twenty-five of his minute men. Father and Brother Will started on the trail.

The Indians, with Jeff and I as their prisoners, went east for about ten miles, then turned north and traveled about the same distance, finally turning west. We crossed the Guadalupe river in a big cedar brake, where now stands the village of Kendalia, a post office being established there some years later to accommodate a considerable number of people who located there to burn the cedar to make charcoal. We traveled until about 2 o'clock that night and camped for a short rest on the Perdernales. Jeff and I were so tired we were almost dead. It was very cold, and the Indians put us down on a wet saddle blanket and tied us with buckskin strings. When they all went to sleep I got a knife out of my pocket, opened it with my teeth, and gave it to Jeff. He cut me loose and then I took the knife and cut the strings which bound him. I took Jeff on my back and started slipping out of camp. I think an Indian must have had one eye open, for he rose up suddenly and when I started to run I fell down in some cedar tops, and lay still. The Indians roused up and began to make a hasty search for us. I could

THE BOY CAPTIVES

easily have made my escape, but would not leave my little brother. When the Indians found us they took us back and chugged us down on that cold, wet, frosty saddle blanket, and we soon fell asleep, for we were utterly exhausted. We did not get to sleep long, for they soon woke us up. We could hear roosters crowing down on the creek.

Off we went again, going northwest. About 9 o'clock that morning they killed a cow, cut her open and began to eat on her like a pack of dogs. She had a bag of milk and they cut into it. The blood and milk mixed together, and they motioned me to drink it, but I shook my head, and an Indian dragged me by the ears and stuck my head down into the milk and tried to make me drink it. Then they would drink it to show me how good it was. But it didn't look good to me. The Indians made no fire and ate the meat raw.

On we went. Jeff and I had nothing to eat Sunday and Monday. On Tuesday they killed another cow. They had placed Jeff and I on a flat rock, about fifteen feet away, and when they cut into that cow we were watching like dogs for our part. They cut out a piece of liver and pitched it to us. I grabbed it from Jeff, as if it were the heart of a big red watermelon. Jeff got the next chunk. And it really was good. The Indians laughed to see us eat that raw liver.

THE BOY CAPTIVES

After we started on we ran into a bunch of wild horses, and the Indians formed a circle around them and roped one. They soon had a hackamore (headstall) on him and wanted us boys to ride him. An Indian who held the horse made signs for me to come and get on. I tried to tell him that the horse would throw me off, but they were in a hurry and had no time to argue about the matter, so he reached down and picked up a stick of wood and hit me on the head with it. It knocked me down, and when I got up the Indian pointed to the horse and I went onto him. Jeff was placed up behind me, and a rope was tied to our feet and passed under the horse and tied to our feet on the opposite side. When we were tied securely the horse was turned loose in the bunch and they started driving us on our way. We did not go far before we came to where a man was making rails. Some of the Indians slipped up and shot him. That was the first man I ever saw killed.

Then on we went again, and after traveling a few miles we saw an old man coming along, smoking his pipe leisurely, with a bridle in his hand, and an old flopped hat on his head. The Indians concealed themselves and lay in wait for him, and when he came near they let fly a number of arrows, one of which struck him in the leg. He turned and ran, with the

THE BOY CAPTIVES

Indians after him. He lost his bridle, hat and pipe, as he almost flew, and outran the Indians. He ran to Fredericksburg, where he had the arrow cut out, I was afterwards told.

Next morning about daylight we passed a ranch house. It seems there had been a dance at this house the night before, but most of the people had gone home from there. A few horses were still tied near the yard gate, and the Indians rode up and got them. When we were about three hundred yards from the house, one of the Indians tried to ride one of the horses, but the animal was frightened and threw him off. The Indian did not understand a white man's saddle, but when they caught the horse and brought him up the Indian mounted and rode him.

We next came to the Llano river, which we crossed, and on the other side we found the grass to be high and very dry. The Indians knew there would be Rangers following them soon. They had spy glasses with them, and would frequently look back to see if they could discover any pursuers. They finally decided to split up into two bunches, one bunch taking Jeff with them, and I going with the other crowd. As we went along they put fire to the high grass in order to blot out the trail, and to confuse Captain Sansom's dogs, which we had heard about daylight on this morning.

THE BOY CAPTIVES

Captain Schreiner's men, so I was told after I came back, were trying to flank the Indians on the west and head them off. For two days the Captain could tell about where we were by the dogs, and the fire and smoke made in trying to obliterate the trail. When Father and Captain Sansom came to where the fire had started they were puzzled, and lost fully half a day in trying to pick up the trail.

I am enabled to give this information, because I was with the Indians and observed all they did, and when I was released five years later, and talked to men who were in the chase, they told me all about how they endeavored to overtake us. The Indians were shrewd and experienced in eluding the white men. When we reached a high peak near the San Saba river they spent some time scanning the country for miles around, to discover signs of pursuit. While there they all took a smoke, and offered me tobacco, too, but I was too hungry to accept. I began to think they had quit eating altogether. Leaving this elevation we went into a long draw, which was very brushy. Here half of them dismounted and began to string their bows. They went slipping away half stooped, and were gone about half an hour. When they returned one of them came to me with two pieces of skin, and motioned to me to tie them on a shield I was holding. I thought

THE BOY CAPTIVES

they were pieces of black calf skin, but I soon discovered they were human scalps. They had waylaid and killed two white men and had brought back these scalps as trophies of their bravery.

From there we went on a few miles and stopped, and the Indians began to dig a hole in the ground. At first I could not understand what they were up to, but when they made a fire in the hole, and made a lot of smoke, I understood they were preparing to send up smoke signals to locate the other band of Indians, with whom Jeff was with. The signal was soon answered, about ten miles away. We rode all that evening and came to a point where we crossed the river, and there on the other side we found the other band waiting for us. And there was Jeff, too, and he looked all right. The waiting Indians had some fresh colt meat, half cooked, but it was good and tender, and I filled up.

The next morning we again crossed the river, and discovered two cowboys, coming up the river, and the Indians laid a trap for them. Jeff and I were on the same horse, at this time, and as I saw those young men coming, and knowing what was going to happen, I got nervous and wanted to cry out and warn them, but I knew it would not be safe for myself and my little brother. As the cowboys rode into the trap, the Indians opened fire on them and killed both of

THE BOY CAPTIVES

their horses. The cowboys promptly returned the fire, killing one Indian and badly wounding another, before the Indians knew what was coming behind them, so they left the dead Indian, and hurried away from the scene. The wounded Indian, with a bullet hole through his shoulder, was able to proceed with the party, and finally recovered.

On we went until we reached open country, when the band stopped to look back. With the aid of their field glasses they could see the Rangers coming on their trail. Although I could not see the Rangers, I knew from the actions of the Indians that we were being pursued, and I was in high hopes that we would be overtaken before we had gone much further. One old Indian, evidently noticing the interest I was taking in the excitement, took me by the neck, placed a field glass up to my eyes, and pointed back the way we had come. I had to look for a few seconds before I could locate anything, but finally I could see three different bunches of men coming towards us. They looked like small specks moving along. The Rangers saw us about that same time, so I learned afterwards. After talking together a little while, two Indians took Jeff and two took me, then the others all rode off in different directions, putting fire to the grass behind them as they went.

THE BOY CAPTIVES

We rode all day, each fellow by himself, and traveled for many miles, when we came to a chalky bluff, where we found three or four of the party already there waiting for us. About sundown the other Indians began coming in from every side. Then they formed in line, two standing on their horses, while the others passed between them. This was done in order to count them. There were now twenty-four in the party, one of the original number having been killed in the fight with the cowboys. Starting out from there we traveled until midnight, then stopped to rest, but the Indians did not make a fire. They gave Jeff and I a prairie chicken, which had been roasted, for our supper. We ate the chicken, and then fell over on the grass and were soon asleep.

When the party composed of Captain Sansom and his Rangers, Captain Schreiner and his Minute Men, and the party of citizens came to where the Indians had divided and fired the grass on the prairie, they lost our trail. The blood hounds could not trail us on account of the fire, and the Indians had scattered in every direction. They lost nearly all of that day trying to pick up the trail, so Captain Sansom called the dogs off and directed that a man take each dog up in the saddle and carry him, while they had a little daylight left in which to travel. Then the Rangers went

THE BOY CAPTIVES

east ten miles, north ten miles, then west about six miles, and that put them out of the burnt grass region. The whites were forced to camp overnight, however, and it was near sundown the next day when they found where the Indian party had come together. Father suggested that they camp for supper, give care to the dogs, rest the horses, and then follow the trail all night. This they did, and expected to overtake the Indians at daylight the next morning.

At about three o'clock in the morning Jeff and I were awakened, and found the Indians ready to go. Every little while we could hear the baying of the blood hounds on our trail. The Indians knew what that meant for they had been chased before. With the approach of daylight we left camp in single file. One of the Indians remained behind. He had some small pouches filled with skunk musk, which he poured along on our trail, so when the dogs got there they could not follow. That skunk musk put them out of service for several miles. Father told me afterwards that they lost half a day on that account, as they could only follow our horses' tracks.

By this time the news of our captivity had reached the troops at Ft. Concho, and the commanding officer of the post had placed troops in a rainbow, east and west of Fort Concho. His idea was to intercept the

THE BOY CAPTIVES

Indians in their flight northward. The soldiers were placed in squads of twenty-five and within sight of each other. At night guards rode from camp to camp. This cordon of troops extended for many miles and it was considered impossible for the Indians to get through, and if they turned back the Rangers were sure to catch them or head them off.

Father and the Rangers knew there were several thousand soldiers in front, waiting for the Indians, and the men following decided to crowd them as fast as possible. My brother-in-law, Sam Lane, who was along with the Rangers, said that when the Indians found themselves in a close place they would turn us boys loose for the Rangers to pick us up while the Indians made their getaway. He had followed a band once before which had a captured boy, and when they came in sight the Indians wrapped the boy in a red blanket and placed him in the trail. When the men reached him the boy was sound asleep.

When we arrived up in that open country, perhaps five miles southeast of Fort Concho, the Indians sent spies on ahead, and when these spies would return the band would bunch close together and chatter. I knew there was something stirring, from their actions, although they did not seem excited. I concluded that the spies had discovered more Rangers ahead, so I

THE BOY CAPTIVES

CLINTON L. SMITH   JEFFERSON D. SMITH

walked up to a big Indian, who had a black star tattooed on his breast, and pointed to his gun and said,
"Boom!" They all laughed.

That was about three o'clock in the afternoon. The
Indians then started back a little southwest, and went
down into a little ravine, keeping their spies on the
high points nearby with the field glasses. I never knew
where these Indians obtained these field glasses, but
during my captivity I often saw field glasses in possession of Indians, and they seemed to appreciate the
value of them. I suppose they obtained them from
the same sources that furnished guns and ammunition.

We were, I suppose, about ten miles from the fort
when we stopped until night, then we moved toward
the fort. The Indians kept very close together, only
riding ahead, until we reached the Concho river, on
the opposite side of which was Fort Concho. Two or
three of the Indians were sent across the river to spy
out the situation, while the rest remained on the banks
of the river. Everything was quiet and still while we
awaited the return of the spies. Soon they came back,
and a whispered conversation was held, and we began a stealthy movement. The fort, having sent nearly
all of the troops out to check this band of Indians, had
neglected to place guards close in around the fort, and

THE BOY CAPTIVES

the Indians were shrewd enough to discover that fact, so we crossed the river and rode up quite near the fort. I could see the lights burning in the quarters, as it was about 10 o'clock when we passed there. Soon we had escaped the net spread for us, and were hurrying forward, in the lead again.

When Father and the Rangers came to where the Indians had doubled back on their trail for a short ways, they lost the trail and did not find it again until near noon the next day. When they followed on they were amazed to discover that the Indians had crossed the river at the fort and were gone, with almost a whole day's gain on them.

They all now felt that the race was lost. They had chased those Indians from Dripping Springs, in Comal county, to Fort Concho, a distance of nearly two hundred miles and they felt that they must abandon the pursuit. The soldiers were called in, and the Rangers and Minute Men, as well as most of the citizens, turned back. There were twelve men, however, who would not turn back, but were determined to follow on and rescue us. These men were my father, Henry Smith, my two brothers-in-law, Sam Lane and Jack Cravey, my brother Will Smith, Mr. Holsinger, the Kelly brothers, Joe Tate, Bill Nichols, Louis Deets, and Billy Holloway.

THE BOY CAPTIVES

The Indians, knowing they had gained a good start on the whites, did not travel so very fast. When we came to a small pond they made camp, and sent me to gather some wood, a short distance away. One of the smart aleck spies, who was on guard, amused himself by shooting arrows into the air and causing them to drop near me, and I had to dodge them until I was well nigh exhausted. The Indians all laughed at me, but for me it was no laughing matter, to have those arrows descending within just a few inches of my head. When he quit shooting I picked up the wood, and we soon had a good roast.

We traveled on and were soon in the buffalo range. The first buffalo we saw I did not know what they were. Late in the day they ran onto one and roped it. It was about two years old. They tied the animal down and put Jeff and I on its back, then turned it loose, and danced in high glee to see us try to stay with it. It did not pitch very hard, but I fell off. Jeff, with his fingers in the wool on his hump, clung on like a cat. I was afraid it would run off with him, so I took after the buffalo, when a big Indian passed me and roped it again. I did not know the thing would fight, so I ran up to it, and it turned and butted me back about fifteen feet, knocking the breath out of me. I rolled over and when I came to the Indians were laughing at me,

THE BOY CAPTIVES

while the blood was running from my nose and mouth. I was learning the wild savage life pretty fast, but it was in a rather tough way.

When Father and his men reached this lonely little pond of water, which was surrounded by low, blue-looking hills, they found the camp which we had left the day before. Father found here one of Jeff's little shoes, with blood on it. He picked it up and began crying, telling his men, "They have killed my boys, for here is Jeff's shoe with blood on it." The blood, however, was caused by the big shields, which Jeff was forced to carry, rubbing the skin off of his leg. The chief had pulled the shoe off and thrown it away. Father and his party were now about two hundred and forty miles from home, had no bread, or coffee, and only meat to eat, and their horses were almost given out, so the men talked Father into turning back, for the Indians had fully fifty miles head start of them. Father consented to turn back, and carried the shoe home with him. He also had a part of my old blue jacket, which he had picked up away back on the Llano river, where one of the Indians had taken it off of me and threw it down.

When the Indians began to get into a hilly region they went to a cave, where they had cached a lot of saddles, blankets, arrows, etc., which they must have

THE BOY CAPTIVES

hidden there when they started on their trip. From here on Jeff and I had an old pack saddle to ride on. We traveled on northwest until we came to some high points, or hills. Here we came to an old Indian trail, but did not know just how old it was until we went up on some of the higher points, where the Indians found small stones placed in the shape of the moon. These stones, I learned from the Indians afterwards, indicated the phase of the moon at the time the stones were arranged in this order. There was also a line of small stones indicating the direction taken by the party who placed them there. Our captors kept following these signs, of various kinds, until we arrived in the Sorneapo Mountains. (The reader will observe that where I give names of mountains or regions in this narrative, it will be as I leaned the names from the Indians. Prior to my captivity, nor since, have I studied the geography of this country.) This was where we overtook the main tribe. There were over two thousand of them camped here, awaiting, the return of our band.

OUR INITIATION INTO THE TRIBE
I cannot express the mingled feelings I had as we approached this great horde of savages, whose camp extended for miles. As we came in sight they began

THE BOY CAPTIVES

to whoop and yell and shoot. Shrill screaming squaws came running toward us crying, "Lelo! lelo! lela!" which means to "shed blood of those they have to fight." We entered the camp, and the returning warriors were given a great reception. A great feast was given, consisting of horse, mule, and buffalo meat.

When they capture a new boy the Comanches always try him out the next day by making him fight an Indian boy. One of the chiefs took charge of Jeff and me. The next day a ring was prepared for a big event. The Indians were all dressed up and painted. I was also painted and had a pretty string of beads placed around by neck. The Indian chief led me to the ring, and I thought they were going to kill me there, but I saw the squaws coming with an Indian boy about my size, all painted up, so I surmised that there was to be a scrap in which I was to participate, and I did not know whether to fight him or not. They put us both in the ring. The Indian boy ran at me and knocked me down. When I got up, he did it again, and then jumped on me and beat me. He was pulled off by the chief. I did not know what to do. The chief took me by the hand and led me back to camp. He tried to tell me something, but I could not understand. Finally he found that I could speak a little Spanish, then he told me in that language that he wanted me to whip that

THE BOY CAPTIVES

Indian boy so he could win a lot of good horses from those old squaws. He took good care of me for two days, then everything was fixed up again. Jeff was also matched with another boy of his size, but I did not see his fight.

When the time came for our second fight a large number of Indians gathered around, and the squaws were there with their hero, the champion of the fight two days before, and as the Indians were inveterate gamblers, bets were placed on the outcome of the scrap. My chief was there, dressed in beads and pretty feathers. He wore a cap on his head which was decorated with gaudy feathers, the streamer reaching to the ground, and he had a black star tattooed on his breast. Black is the emblem of death. As he walked to the ring by my side he carried a tomahawk in one hand and a pistol in the other. The squaws set up their cry, "Lelo! Lelo! Lelo!" and the chief pushed me forward, gave a war-whoop, and the Indian boy and I went together, hitting right and left. Soon the Indian boy knocked me down and jumped on me. As he did so I threw my arms around him and buried my teeth into his flesh with a death grip. He struggled and tried to get loose, but I hung on. Then he began to howl, but I did not release my hold. The squaws started to separate us, but the chief pointed his pistol

THE BOY CAPTIVES

toward them and made them stand back. The excitement was great, for it was becoming a critical time for the squaws' favorite. The Indians fired many shots into the air, and many were yelling and laughing. Then two Indians entered the ring and tried to pull me loose from my adversary, but I held on, so they began choking me, and I was almost strangled before I would let go.

The chief took me by the hand, patted me on the head, and said, "Bravo!" He had won the horses, and I was now very much in his favor. His name was Tosacowadi, or Leopard Cat. He had a son whose name was Monewostuki, and he gave me to understand that I was to be his son too, and he wanted me and Monewostuki to be brothers, and that my name was to be Bac-ke-ca-cho, (end of a rope.) Brother Jeff was also given an Indian name, Na-i-flink.

We remained in camp at this place about two weeks, and then had a dance over the scalps our party had brought back with them. It was a gala occasion for savage merriment, and there had been much preparation for it. Some of the Indians dressed to represent various wild animals and fowls, the deer, bear, buffalo, fowls, eagles and turkeys. There were about six hundred dancers, with four hundred mounted warriors and many hundreds of spectators. The dance started

THE BOY CAPTIVES

about 9 o'clock one morning, and the participants danced through the entire length of the encampment, about three miles. The chief kept Jeff and I on horses, and he rode in the lead with his scalps attached to his tomahawk. All of the savages were singing, and when they came to a certain part of the song they would begin shouting and yelling. Of course to us two boys,

MRS. CAROLINE COKER   MRS. AMANDA LANE
Sisters to Clint and Jeff Smith

unused to a celebration of this kind, it was a strange and horrifying sight to see those Indians capering about as they did, and we looked on in wonderment and could only guess at what they meant. The dance lasted two days, each morning and afternoon. The Indians had their odd drums, tin pans and wooden whistles to furnish "music," and no doubt thought they were having a good time. As for Jeff and I, we would much rather have been at home with our own people,

THE BOY CAPTIVES

but that was out of the question.

It was then about the month of May, grass was fine and buffalo were fat. We never saw nor heard of those men from Texas, who were following us. Soon we drifted on north, and came to a little creek in the bend of which was about one hundred acres. Here I saw great piles of bleaching bones of horses. The Indians pointed out to me some holes wherein lay human bones and piles of empty cartridge shells, and said, "Indians kill gringos." I think this gruesome spot was the battlefield where a Captain Rogers and his troops were massacred some years before. The Indians said they fought for five days and nights and killed them all.

At that time there were tribes of Indians scattered from Texas to Montana, through Oregon and back to Arizona, and through all to the intervening territory. They spoke different languages, but could always manage to understand each other by use of the sign language. I have met many wild Indians of other tribes, with whom I could talk by signs, although I was a Comanche by adoption.

The first six months I was with the Indians we were not bothered by other tribes, being at peace with most of them, but afterwards we had a hard time fighting, and running to keep out of fights. The Blackfeet In-

THE BOY CAPTIVES

dians began to steal our horses and then war with them began. The Comanches had about six thousand horses, and my chief, Tosacowadi, owned about one hundred of them. I had to herd my chief's horses at night, usually from 2 a.m. until daylight. Each family had horses, some more, some less, than others. They were not all herded together. Sometimes, when on night herding, I would get so sleepy that I would take a rope, tie it to the front of my saddle, then around my waist, and to the back of the saddle. The Indian saddles were made very much like the ordinary packsaddle used many years ago by the early settlers. When I had securely tied myself on I would let the horse graze while I lay over on his shoulder and neck and slept. I would sometimes sleep for hours in this way, and when day light came I would find myself a mile or two from camp. Then I would round up the horses and drive them in. I have been on herd and in the dead hours of the night have seen Blackfeet Indians crawling on their hands and knees, creeping forward to steal, but they were after horses that were staked, and I did not give the alarm so long as they did not bother my chief's horses. Once when we were not on herd, and did not know the Blackfeet were in the country, they made a raid on our horses and stole about three thousand of them, mostly stock horses, but there were a large num-

THE BOY CAPTIVES

ber of our best saddle horses in the lot. We spent most of the next day getting ready to follow them. It was estimated that there were fully eighteen hundred Blackfeet Indians in the band, and the Comanches took the trail with about twelve hundred warriors. They left Jeff in the camp, but took me along to wait on the chief. We overtook the Blackfeet after following them three days, and found them about 9 o'clock in the morning. They had killed about eighty buffalo and were cooking the meat. Perhaps they intended to carry a supply of the meat with them. Some of the Indians were herding the horses, and some were eating. We charged upon them, hoping to give them a scare and recover the horses without a fight, but they would not run, and instead, sprang upon their horses and came meeting us. The battle raged for about six hours, with many braves falling in hand-to-hand combat. Finally our chief, with about a hundred warriors, stampeded the horses, and the Blackfeet were whipped. They fought bravely, but they were not as well equipped with good guns as the Comanches were. While the fight was in progress arrows were falling all around me, and I found one sticking in the back of my saddle when the fight was over.

We stayed there that night, and ate some of the buffalo meat the Blackfeet had cooked. With some

THE BOY CAPTIVES

others I was placed on herd, while other Indians looked after the wounded and dead. Others were sent to the willow bottoms to cut travois poles on which to carry the wounded back to our camp. The Indians would bore holes in one end of these poles, with knives, and would put ropes through them, and tie one on each side of a horse, like a buggy shaft. One end of the pole would drag on the ground behind the horse. Then a buffalo robe or a blanket would be tied across the poles in hammock fashion, and the wounded Indian was placed in this suspended bed and comfortably conveyed to camp. Some of the wounded died on the way. Some would cry for water along the trail. When we came to water the wounded were washed and given water to drink. If any of them bled too freely the hemorrhage would be stopped by packing the wound with grass.

When we reached camp the squaws set up a doleful howl, and cried for a long time afterwards. They would wait until night and then go to the top of some lonely hill and cry and moan for hours. And to emphasize their grief they would take a knife and gash their faces and arms and sometimes their breasts, and when morning came they would return to camp covered with dried and clotted blood.

These Indians, instead of burying their dead, would

THE BOY CAPTIVES

wrap the corpse in a blanket and take it to the peak of a high hill, where they would set up three poles, lashing them together, with the blanketed corpse bound securely to the end, and raise it up as high as possible, the poles being set up in tripod fashion. This was done to protect the dead body from wolves and other animals, until in the course of time the poles rotted down.

Every time we went north we would have trouble with the Blackfeet Indians of Montana, so we drifted west into some very rough mountain region, where we came upon Chief Bosobow's band of Kiowas. There were about five thousand of this tribe in the camp. We saw the village while we were yet a long way off, and had to give signals that we were also Indians. The signal was made in this manner: We formed a long line facing them; their spies assembled in a line parallel to ours; then one Indian rode out in front of our line, and turned and rode about thirty steps to the right; then rode thirty steps to the left; then back to his starting place and stopped. The Kiowa spies did the same, and in this way understood we were friendly Indians, and signaled for us to come on as there was no danger.

When Indians see a camp a long distance off they cannot always tell whether it is other Indians or sol-

THE BOY CAPTIVES

diers. Indians have this sign to guide them. Soldiers do not understand it. If there are but two Indians out on a prairie and they see each other a long way off they have to give this sign. If one does not understand it the other knows he is not a wild Indian.

We remained in the camp of the Kiowas for a long time and had great sport hunting bear. In that region, which must have been the Rocky Mountains, there were many grizzly bear, a few elk and mountain sheep. The Indians told me to always run from a grizzly as they were the worst of the bear kind. The first one I saw I was going after the horses one morning when I met him in a narrow trail. He was only about forty steps from me. He stood straight up when he saw me. When he came down on all fours, I turned my pony towards camp and bade him good-bye. After I stayed with those Indians awhile I became braver and did not fear any kind of a bear. The Indians killed many of them, and would take their teeth and claws and make necklaces of them.

When fall set in we drifted south and went as far as Utah, I suppose it was, as I did not know where I was all the time except by guess.

On our way south we came across a wagon train of immigrants. There were ten or fifteen wagons, with about eight yoke of oxen to the wagon. We had a

THE BOY CAPTIVES

hard fight with these immigrants, and during the scrap I was struck in the face with a charge of small shot. Some of these shot are in my face yet. The Comanches killed all of the men, women and children. They also killed the oxen, cut up the feather beds and emptied the feathers to the wind. They destroyed almost everything. When I was shot I fell off my horse, but was helped to place of safety by an Indian. After the fight the Indians held me down and picked most of the shot out of my face, but they did not get them all. There were a few Indians killed in the fight. After destroying this wagon train and killing the immigrants, we went on south to winter where there was plenty of game and wild honey. That winter the snow was two or three feet at times. I have often lain down to sleep after clearing off a place, and the Indians would cover me with a buffalo robe. Next morning it would be difficult to get up, the snow would be so deep over me. But I would manage to kick out, and thought nothing of it.

When spring came again we went down in Texas, and when the first full moon came around we went out on a big killing and stealing raid. The second chief took about seventy-five warriors, including myself, on this raid. We were all painted up, and no one could have told me from an Indian boy. I do not

THE BOY CAPTIVES

know just where we were, but I remember the ranches were quite a distance apart. We split up in small bunches, I being with a band numbering about fifteen. Every horse we found we would take him. We saw some hogs and the Indians would point to them and say, "White man's meat; no good," and we killed them. We came to a ranch at which there was no one except a woman and two little children. Two horses were tied at the gate. We got them, and tried to get the woman, but she put up a desperate fight. The Indians shot the door full of arrows, and the woman shot the chief in the neck, so we left her alone. We had a time putting a prickly pear poultice on the chief's neck. On this raid we stole about thirty head of horses and were going back to camp when we ran across two men, who, when they discovered us, started to run. I and an Indian stayed with the horses, while the others followed the white men. Soon we heard shooting, and when we came up with the band they had killed both men and scalped them. I saw the Indians cut off their arms and hang them up in trees. We got their horses and saddles, and went on our way. This was the only killing our bunch did on that trip. When we reached our camp we found some of those who started at the same time we did had returned, but some of them never came back, and we supposed they had been

THE BOY CAPTIVES

killed.

We then moved on towards Fort Sill, where the Indians could get more guns and ammunition, and when we got within about 100 miles of that place, a large party of our band left us and went on to Fort Sill for the supplies. While in camp waiting for the return of those who went to the fort, the Indians had all kinds of sports. The Indian boys and I would go in bathing every day, run horse races, rope buffalo calves and ride them, and take wild horses out into deep sand and ride them. I was now pretty well Indianized, and became quite an expert rider.

When the party returned from Fort Sill they were loaded down. The government had given them a full supply. We could now go on another killing and steal-ing expedition, so we drifted back west about five hundred miles, went into camp and had a big dance. A short time afterward a caravan of Mexican traders were discovered coming in from Old Mexico. Our spies met them about fifty miles from our camp, and learned they were loaded with coffee, tobacco, whis-key, etc., all on jacks. They had no guns, so they were told to come to our camp and trade with the Indians. And such trading that took place! Those fool Indians would let the Mexicans pick their mules for a keg of whiskey; ten pounds of coffee was accepted for a

THE BOY CAPTIVES

pack horse, five pounds of tobacco would get a mule, and a buffalo robe would be exchanged for little or nothing. The traders stayed with us two or three weeks. The only way the Indians would let them come into camp was with packs loaded down on jacks, but they would let them take back what they had traded to them.

When the traders had gone one of the spies came in one day and reported that he had seen a bunch of Rangers coming that way. In a few hours there were about fourteen hundred squaws and bucks, all armed and painted up, with horses ready to go. The remainder of the band stayed in camp. I had to go and lead the chief's horse, so if his horse was killed in battle or gave out, he would have another. We went on to meet the Rangers, riding fast most of the day. When we arrived in sight of them we found they were camped by the side of a river, and most of them were out hunting, evidently not expecting an Indian attack. That was our time, the chief said, to make a charge on them. The Indians dashed forward, whooping and yelling, and every one that had a gun was shooting. Away went the Rangers' horses, about one hundred head. Most of them had been tied up, but they broke loose and joined in the stampede. We passed within about two hundred yards of the camp, and the bullets fell

THE BOY CAPTIVES

about us like hail. A few were killed and a few were wounded in our band. I do not know how many of the Rangers were killed in the fight, but we carried the horses away, and thought it was very easily done. We took these horses to our camp and took their shoes off, and this was quite a task. The shoes were removed in order that we would have no trouble in trading them to the Mexicans, who were afraid to trade for horses that had been stolen from Rangers or soldiers for fear the government would take such animals away from them.

This was in 1872, and about one month after we made the raid on the Rangers' camp, we discovered a troop of soldiers coming in our direction, and we pulled out from there and headed for the desert country to get away from them. We were followed for many miles, our spies keeping us informed of the soldiers' movements. The chief said there were too many soldiers in the party for us to fight, and that we would have to keep traveling. We reached a stretch of plains country which it took us four days to cross, to where there was a large lake which the Indians called Utcherbow (Crooked Lake.) Many thousands of buffalo watered at this lake, and other wild game as well. In crossing that dry stretch of country we suffered greatly for water, our only supply, carried in beef

THE BOY CAPTIVES

paunches, having been exhausted the first day or two. We were almost dead with thirst, and it was in the summer time, and when we reached the lake you can imagine our disappointment and distress when we found it was dry. Tons of dead fish, carcasses of buffalo, deer, antelope, and coyotes, covered the dry bed of the lake. We could not turn back, for behind us was a large company of soldiers seeking our lives. Despondently we turned south, and began the most trying march the Indians ever experienced during my captivity. I thought the first day after leaving that dry lake that I would surely die of consuming thirst. The next day the Indians began to kill their horses and drink the blood, but I could not do that. My tongue began to swell and I suffered untold agony. A little water was kept in some buffalo paunches for the babies to drink, and I tried to slip in at night and steal some of it, but it was too well guarded. Late in the evening of the second day after we left the dry lake we saw some tall mountains in the distance and went to them. When we got there we went down into a deep canyon where we found the head spring of a river. I fell off my horse and crawled down to the little running stream and when I began to try to drink the water it would run out at my nose. My tongue and throat was so badly swollen that the water would

THE BOY CAPTIVES

not go down. And most of the Indians were in the same fix. A few of the Indians died and many of them were sick. We stayed for about a month to rest up. Many of the horses died from the effects of this hard trip. We never saw or heard anything more of the soldiers who were pursuing us.

While here we killed lots of buffalo and dried the meat. This was where I killed my first buffalo. I always had to go along on the hunts and carry the meat back to camp on a big mule. He was a good one, and could run like a horse. When the Indians started a bunch of buffalo they soon ran out of sight, and I on my mule was loping along on the trail when I saw a yearling buffalo which had left the herd and turned back. I took after it with only a spear, and ran it down until I came alongside, when I struck it in the ribs with the spear. It did not go very far until it sank down, and I rode up and killed it, skinned it, cut it up in small pieces so I could lift them up on my mule, and when I got him loaded up I did not know where the Indians were. I started for camp, about eight miles off, and when I reached there the chief asked me where the other hunters were and I said: "I do not know. I got lost from them, so I just killed me a buffalo and brought it back." He ran up to me and said "La, la, muy bueno!" and patted me on the back. When I be-

THE BOY CAPTIVES

came older I killed lots of buffalo, but I think that I was prouder of that first buffalo calf than of any I ever killed.

We then drifted on south for a month or more and found a big Apache camp, and we stayed with them for a week or two, trading and gambling. The Apache squaws wore brass rings in their ears, bracelets on their arms, and were altogether different from the Comanches. Nearly every morning they would take their papooses down to the creek and dip them in ice cold water, and I thought it would kill the little fellows.

The Indians would bet on anything, shooting, foot races or horse races. I often rode in their races. They would tie me on a horse hard and fast and tell me to whip him through and try to win the race for them.

BROTHER JEFF SOLD TO GERONIMO

With the Apaches we drifted on south. Geronimo was chief of the Apaches, and he seemed to take a fancy to my little brother Jeff, and bought him from my chief, Tosacowadi, giving a good horse and a lot of powder and lead for him. That is one time I could not help crying. When the trade was made poor little Jeff was tied up and branded like a cow, and he carries the scars of this brand to this day. He was taken

THE BOY CAPTIVES

away and I did not see him again for nearly a year. This was in February, 1873, and in the spring the Indians prepared for another raid south. They took me with them on this raid. By that time my hair had grown long, and I was sunburned so I looked like an Indian, and naturally I was afraid the white people would kill me, but I had to go along with the band to wait on them. Twenty-five of us started out and when we reached the settlements we split up into small bunches, the crowd I accompanied numbering five. We ascended a high mountain and down on the other side we saw a house, and watched there all through the afternoon. We saw an old man take three fine horses out of the stable and take them to water. About 9 o'clock, when everything was still and quiet, and the moon was shinning bright, we crept down near the stable and I and two of the Indians went in to get the horses, the others standing guard. To lead the horses out we had to let down the fence which joined an old log pen. When they let the fence down easy I cut the rope and led one horse out, while an Indian went in to get the others. One Indian was in the way of the horse coming out so he stepped against the old log pen. Unknown to us there was a white man in this log pen watching us, and at this moment he cut down on the nearest Indian and killed him. We turned the horses

THE BOY CAPTIVES

loose and ran for our lives back to where we were to get together again. When all was quiet once more, we hooted like an owl for our missing companion, but received no reply, so we know Tovanty was dead, or he would have answered. We waited until about 2 o'clock in the morning, and then went to a dense cedar brake some miles away. Next day we killed a horse and cooked it and rested and slept for a few hours. We could find no other Indians, so we started for our camp and it took about two weeks hard riding to get there. When we showed up in camp with one of the warriors missing there was great wailing by the squaws. Later on the balance of our party came in, but had had good luck. They had stolen a lot of horses and had taken two scalps. I was severely punished by the Indians. They poured sand in my eyes, and said I ought to have looked into that old log pen.

We moved back eastward where we found all kinds of wild fruit, grapes, sand hill plums, crab-apples, wild sweet potatoes, and various kinds of berries. Here we met with another party of Mexicans, with their trading clothes on. This time they brought with them all kinds of paint, knives, steel with which to make arrow points, and many trinkets. The arrival of the steel in our camp caused a lot of work for we were soon busy making bows and arrows, quivers and lari-

THE BOY CAPTIVES

ats. Among the trinkets brought in were steels for striking fire with flint, and used extensively by the Indians. One method the Indian has, however, of making fire, is to bore a hole in the middle of a sotol stalk, take a dry bois d'arc stick and put powder on a rag and rub all together rapidly, the friction ignites the powder and rag.

Just here I will digress and answer a question asked me very often, and that is how the Indians make their pipes, which every chief and most warriors have. Usually they make their pipes out of soapstone, which they were able to procure in various sections of the country. It is easy to fashion and answers as well as clay or meerschaum. Sometimes these pipes are artistically graven, and are very pretty in design. When smoking the Indians, ten or twelve of them, seat themselves in a circle, and after filling the pipe with tobacco, the chief takes a draw at it and passes it on to the next Indian, and it goes the round. Visitors to the wigwam of the chief or other Indians are invited to smoke "the pipe of peace, " and with much solemnity the smoking goes on.

Another thing made by the Indians which attracted my boyish interest was a device used for gambling, which I would term as dice. Some times while smoking they would indulge in gambling with these so-

THE BOY CAPTIVES

called dice. They made these dice from small square blocks of wood, each of the four sides being painted a different color, red, blue, black and white, and in "rolling" these blocks they would bet on the colors. The Indian is an inveterate gambler, and nothing seemed to suit the bucks better than to sit for hours and play with these blocks, while the squaws and I would have to cook meat for them.

The Indians are as a rule very superstitious, and one of their superstitions was in regard to the manner in which they drank water. They believed the proper way to drink it was to lap it with their tongue, like a dog, or carry it to their mouth with the hand, and they would not drink from a cup while standing up, but would always squat down. Other superstitions and customs they had were many. They would never drag a rope up to camp, or let a rope drag from their horses, as they claim that snakes crawl to camp at night along a track made by a rope drag. When a baby boy is born in camp they paint a black spot on the door of the wigwam, which means "brave". They do not name the child until he is about two years old, preferring to wait to see if he is a sleepy-headed child. They never put sticks of wood across the fire, but always put one end on at a time. When they kill a rattlesnake to eat they always cut off a portion six inches from the head

THE BOY CAPTIVES

and six inches from the end of the tail before roasting it. Rattlesnake meat is white and very delicious when properly cooked. The Indians never shake hands when meeting, but instead they point a finger at each other. They never wear the clothing of white people whom they kill, although other members of the tribe may wear such clothing. They never break their horses until they pull the wild hairs from around the horse's eyes. They always train their boys to use the bow and arrow with either hand. When they killed a buffalo they always ate raw the kidneys, liver and paunch. If it was a buffalo cow giving milk, they would cut into the bag and drink the milk. If they killed a sucking calf, which had never eaten grass, they would cut into its stomach to get the milk contained therein, and considered this milk a rare delicacy. They would catch dry land terrapins and put them in the fire alive to roast them, and with a horn spoon they would eat the contents of the shell. Sometimes I would be so hungry that I was glad to get a roasted terrapin to eat. I had by this time become to all intents and purposes a wild Indian, and did not stand on ceremony or polite manners among this tribe of savages, whose tastes and habits I had fully adopted.

We resumed our ramblings and went on northwest with no seeming particular destination in view. We

THE BOY CAPTIVES

met up with thousands of Indians of different tribes, among them being the Caraways, a very wild and savage tribe. We drifted along for quite a while, having a good time killing all kinds of game. At times we would camp for several weeks and engage in making fine beaded moccasins, dressing buckskin, making buffalo robes, lariats, saddles, arrows, quivers and bows. Finally we reached a region which I believe was in Western Kansas, where white people had begun to settle and put in small farms here and there. The Indians killed many of these settlers and carried away their horses. After keeping this up for awhile we went on over to Nebraska, being followed by a party of these settlers, who overtook us on the Little Platte river, where we had quite a fight and killed a lot of them. In this fight the Indians lost about sixty warriors. We had a hard time getting our wounded away from there, but we managed it somehow, and went on into Wyoming to the Lamo Hills (I use the Indian name for these hills) to rest up and doctor our wounded. Usually I had to help in dressing the wounds of the warriors, that is I would have to help hold them, and it was generally like "hogging" down a steer to doctor him for worms.

As I grew older my chief pushed me to the front with the warriors, and it seemed the longer I stayed

THE BOY CAPTIVES

with them the more fights they had, and I was forced
to do my share of the fighting.

In due course of time we started south again, and
drifted along until we came to a big river, where we
encamped, and sent out spies to investigate the lay of
the land. The spies returned and reported that there
were some settlers on scattering ranches, and further
on down the river was a little town. The chief gave
orders to assemble one hundred warriors to make a
raid on the town, and try to steal all the horses without a fight if possible. I was selected to go with the
band on this raid, although I did not want to go. We
traveled for three or four days, and when we came
near the little town we waited until night to make our
raid. That night the moon shone brightly, although a
bank of heavy clouds was rising in the northwest. We
split up into small bunches, and stealthily made our
way around the town, and succeeded in stealing a good
many horses. I saw three or four lamps burning in
little homes in that town, and perhaps I should have
made an attempt to escape at that time from the Indians, but I had been with them for some time and had
become so attached to my chief and members of the
tribe I could not muster courage enough to try to make
my getaway. My association with them for so long
had impressed me with the feeling that I could

THE BOY CAPTIVES

never make a successful attempt to escape, and the desire to do so had about subsided anyway. I considered myself an Indian, and an Indian I would be.

We made this raid without firing a shot, and drove the horses back to our camp, and immediately moved on down toward Texas, finally reaching the headwaters of rivers leading to the plains. Here we found plenty of prickly pear apples, cedar berries, haws, persimmons and some game which included bear and buffalo which had drifted south at that time. We also met up with about 300 Comanche Indians under old Hicho, the chief, and camped with them for awhile. We had several war dances and horse races, and in a few days some Mexican traders came to our camp with about 200 jack loads of supplies, hardtack, sugar, coffee, tobacco, whiskey and mescal, and the trading was lively. The Indians traded good horses, mules and buffalo robes for what the Mexicans brought in. The Indian boys and I had a great deal of fun riding the Mexicans' jacks, which had only been broken to carry packs. After the Mexicans left us we drifted on down the river, and we went into New Mexico, killing and stealing. We camped about twenty miles from a town, when our spies came in and reported that a large party of men were following our trail, so in a few hours we were all packed up and the squaws and

THE BOY CAPTIVES

children were sent down the river, while the warriors, all painted and well armed, dropped back and hid in caves and among rocks to await the coming of the white men. They rode into the ambuscade and were nearly all massacred. I did not see this fight, as I had been sent away with the squaws. The Indians, near the little town above mentioned, captured two Mexican boys and a white girl. The boys were about seven and thirteen years old respectively and the girl was about nine. The older boy stole a big roan horse from the Indians one night and escaped. He was followed for three days, but was not overtaken. At that time in that country you could follow a horse's track all day in a gallop, as the grass was so dry every time the horse put his foot down it would crush the grass and leave a plain print. The little girl was kindly treated by her captors, and was still with them when I left. These Indians had about eighteen captive boys and girls, some of whom had been with them for years. All of the boys over twelve years old were compelled to go with them on their stealing raids.

When we came down to the Pecos river region in Texas the Indians secured some large mesquite thorns and stuck them through my ears, and left the thorns sticking there for some time, to make holes in which to wear rings. Eventually these holes grew up, but

THE BOY CAPTIVES

the holes Brother Jeff had punched in his ears remained open and he can still wear earrings in them. The chief turned north with the big bend and ordered seventy-five braves to go east on a raid, and I was compelled to go with them. At that time, of course, I did not know where we were, but since I came back to civilization I have been convinced that this was in the Pecos country. We rode for three or four days and came upon a Mexican camp of sheepherders. We waylaid them and killed the herders, took their pistols and some dried meat and stole their horses. This was probably on the West Nueces. We then split up into small bunches, part of them going back to the main body and I with twelve others going on to the Frio river. This band of Indians saw an old man riding along on a good pony and attacked him. He shot at them as they came on, but failed to hit any of them, and before he could reload his gun they killed him. We then went on until we came to a little creek on the bank of which was located a small hut, and an old woman was there milking a cow in a little pen near the hut. Some of the Indians slipped up and killed her with spears. This happened about sundown, and we turned northeast and went up on the head of the Sabinal and traveled until next day, when we went into a cedar brake to rest and cook something to eat.

THE BOY CAPTIVES

We killed a calf and roasted it. My horse was so tender-footed he could hardly go. The next day we went over into the Llano river valley, and while spying around we came upon three men, who fought desperately, but the Indians killed all of them. One of the Indians of our party, old Cashon, was badly wounded. We tried to take him along with us, but he was shot in the breast, and we were forced to put him in a cave under a bluff, and leave him there. The last I saw of him he was begging for water, and I would have stayed and helped him, but as we were in a settled country it would have been folly, for we would have been discovered and killed by the white people. We traveled until late that night, and after sleeping and resting a short while we were up early and started on. The Indians stole three horses and I got one of them, leaving my old worn-out pony there. We rode hard going northwest. We would travel at night, using the stars for a guide. I was completely worn-out, had a big carbuncle on my neck as large as an egg, my eyes were almost closed for want of sleep, and I had great sores on my legs from rubbing against the old pack-saddle. The ranchmen were following on our trail and pressing us close, and we began to think they would overtake us before we could make our getaway. I was then about thirteen years old, and the hardship

THE BOY CAPTIVES

of this ride was telling on my strength. But we succeeded in throwing our pursuers off our track, and after riding about twenty days we got back to the main band of Indians, who had gone up into the Panhandle after we left them, and were camped on Wolf Creek. There was weeping and wailing among the squaws when we told how we had to leave Cashon in a cave on the Llano river.

We then went further north to the buffalo range, where we found thousands upon thousands of buffalo in immense herds. We camped on a little river, the banks of which were from six to eight feet high. One day the Indians went out to kill buffalo, and after they had been gone about four hours I saw the Indians in camp running towards an elevated place some two hundred yards off. I hastened toward camp and the Indians hollered to me to look out for the buffalo were coming. I looked north and saw what I first took for a black cloud rising, but soon discerned that it was a buffalo stampede. It was a grand sight to see those huge animals on the run, with about fifty Indians trying to flank them and turn the leaders away from the camp. Indians on the fastest horses were in the lead, shooting and yelling, but they could not turn the main body. When the herd struck the camp, down went the wigwams and the buffalo went plunging on with the

THE BOY CAPTIVES

tents on their head and backs. When they reached the creek the leaders fell over the banks and the others piled up on them until it was almost level with buffalo. Many were killed, as were also several horses which were staked near the camp. They made a clean sweep through our camp and very little was left that was worth picking up, and it took the Indians a month or more to get fixed up again from this misfortune. Buffaloes have so much hair in their faces they cannot see very well in front and will run over anything that gets in their way. The Indians are always afraid of buffaloes stampeding and running into their camp, as there is danger of the squaws and children being run over and killed, and they keep them turned away as much as possible.

Some time after this I was permitted to go out with a party of Indians to kill buffalo. I had an old pistol and was riding a very pretty spotted horse. When the chase started I picked out a long slim cow and after running her for about five hundred yards I got close enough to shoot, and wounded her so badly she turned and came back towards me. I stopped and as she came on I fired at her again, but missed her, and as she came on I turned to get out of her way when she struck my horse in the flank with her horn, hooking him down, and as he fell he caught me under his neck, in such a

THE BOY CAPTIVES

position I could not easily extricate myself. My horse died with his head across me. The enraged buffalo kept hooking him for awhile and then ran away. After much difficulty I wormed my way out and walked to camp, and when I told the chief what had happened he only said: "You are too little to kill buffalo. Don't try that any more." I had to wait until the other Indians came back to go with me to find my saddle. In that country all of the landscape looked alike. There were no trees nor hills to guide me, but we found the dead horse and the saddle after quite a search. After that I had to go along with the Indians to carry the meat back.

We then moved on into the sand hills, where I have seen the wind blow hard for five or six days at a time without ceasing, and the sand would drift for many miles and form hills. I have seen cottonwood trees in the lowlands almost covered by the sand. We had to move our camp frequently to keep from being buried by the sand. We passed on through the sand hills and headed for the Wyoming territory to spend the summer. One day the spies came in and reported seeing several thousand soldiers moving north, so the chief said we would hide in the mountains. Other spies were sent out to watch the movements of the soldiers and learn if possible where they were going. In a day

THE BOY CAPTIVES

or two these spies returned and reported that the supposed troops of soldiers were only great herds of buffalo going north. So, our uneasiness and alarm gave way and we remained in camp enjoying ourselves, for our horses were fat and the Indians had plenty to eat. In the course of a few weeks the Blackfeet Indians began to give us trouble by trying to steal our horses, and we had to night-herd the droves. It usually happened that I was on herd the first part of the night. The chief finally decided that the camp should be moved further west, and so he rode through the village and made the announcement. We had fought the Blackfeet before this, and naturally did not want trouble with them. So we pulled out from there and traveled three or four days and made camp. The next morning we found that a colt had been killed by a bear during the night, and was partly devoured. Some of the Indians took the trail of the bear and followed it to some cliffs, where the dogs bayed it under a big rock. They killed the bear, skinned it, and brought the carcass to camp. The animal's claws were over two inches long, and the Indian who got these claws placed them on a necklace, and was very proud of his trophy.

From here we went on to a little creek and camped and turned the horses loose to graze. Next morning

THE BOY CAPTIVES

when I was sent out to look after the horses, in passing through a small cedar brake, I came face-to-face with a big grizzly bear. The trail was too narrow to pass him, and I did not know just what to do. When the bear rose up on his hind feet, sniffing the air, my little paint horse suddenly turned around, and we left there in a great big hurry. When I reached camp I told the chief about seeing the great big bear, and some of them went back with me to the place, but he had disappeared and we never found him.

We resumed our journey westward, traveling by easy stages for a long time, finally reaching some high, rocky mountains, where there was not much grass. I saw animals on those mountains which looked like sheep, but they would get up on rugged precipices. When the dogs would get after them, those animals would jump off of cliffs and never get injured. Traveling on further we came to some more Indians who were living in little huts. This tribe cultivated gardens and had plenty of vegetables and fruits. They did not roam about like other tribes, but were permanently located along the banks of little creeks. I do not know what tribe they belonged to, for they could only talk to us in the sign language. They treated us kindly and gave us such food as we wanted. It seemed to me that all of the running streams in that

THE BOY CAPTIVES

region flowed north, and it was all new to me. I have no idea where we were, or what state that was in. We did not fancy that region so we traveled southwest until we came to a river which flowed south. Here we camped for awhile, and while there we found a lot of wild horses. We succeeded in capturing about twenty-five of these horses and among the lot was a beautiful slender animal of buckskin color, with black mane and tail, and very wild. The Indians hackamored him and kept him staked until he would lead. Then they made me ride him. To prevent me from falling off while the animal was pitching, they tied my feet under his belly, and with a rope on his nose for me to hold, they turned him loose, gave a yell, and the horse began pitching, and right here I want to tell you he did not slight the job. He was the most rambunctious bronco I ever rode. He pitched all over the landscape until he was almost exhausted, but he could not get me off, although he had managed to get me turned head downward and hanging under his belly. He tried to kick me, but fortunately his hoofs could not reach me. Then he decided to run, and the Indians had to run him down and rope him. The rascals had a world of fun out of the performance, but it was not funny to me, for I was pretty well battered up and considerably bruised. Later they put a saddle on the horse,

THE BOY CAPTIVES

and made me ride him again. He did not throw me, but he pitched so hard he nearly popped my head off. We succeeded in gentling all of those wild horses, that is, gentled them as Indians gentle horses, and which I would call about half-broken, and resumed our drifting toward the southwest. We climbed high rocky divides and traveled for about a month, until we began to get out on the desert, so we turned east and tried to go to the line of Arizona. Here we camped for some time, and about three hundred warriors went off on a stealing raid, but I did not go with them, for I had to herd horses and carry wood and water for the squaws. The raiding band was not gone very long before they returned bringing with them some good horses and a small herd of cattle. The cattle were immediately killed and the meat was dried to carry with us. Dried meat will keep for months, and the Indians packed it in this way; They would make a kind of a box out of rawhide, two or three feet long and about twenty inches wide, so it will fit a pack-saddle. They cut the meat thin and hang it up to dry and when packing they fold the dry sheets of meat and put it in these rawhide boxes and place a box on each side of the packsaddle, and carry it with them. Many is the time I have slyly loosened the string on a box and swiped some of that dried meat. It was real

THE BOY CAPTIVES

good, and very palatable the way the Indians prepared it. I never lost an opportunity to steal something to eat, especially dried meat or hardtack. When in camp the Indians would not let me enter their tents except in the day time, so I would wait until they were asleep and then I would slip in and help myself to hardtack, which looked like a biscuit but were so very hard they have to be wet before you could eat them. Indians kept missing hardtack, and naturally suspected me, but I was hard to catch. One day, however, an old squaw found me at a spring eating hardtack, and she reported me to the chief, who called me up and said: "Ba-ke-ta-cho, I want you to tell me how you managed to steal those cakes, with all of us near, and you have not clothes on which to hide them, after we have been trying for so long to catch you." I told him I stuck them under my arms, and then showed him how easily I could conceal them. He was greatly pleased, and said; "You will never starve. Po-ho-to, give him two more for being so wise."

We next headed for Texas, and after drifting along for three or four weeks we met with Geronimo's band and camped together. When I went to a spring after a vessel of water I found my brother Jeff there getting water also. I knew him at once, and hugged and kissed him joyously. We played there and talked together so

THE BOY CAPTIVES

long that night came on before we realized how time was passing. When I went back with the water, my foster-mother, the chief's wife, was going to whip me. I told her I had found my brother at the spring, he who had been sold to the Apaches, and I could not bear the thought of leaving him. My eyes filled with tears and my voice trembled when I told her this. The chief was in the tent and heard me, and he came out and said "Lepia, you must not whip Be-ke-ca-cho. Poor little papoose." So he sent Ka-ha-co, another squaw over to the Apaches to get Geronimo to bring Jeff and come over for a long talk. The squaws put a lot of buffalo ribs on the fire to roast and when they came over we had a merry time. The Indians made Jeff and I hug and kiss each other, and sing and dance for them. We knew only a part of the song, "Old Dan Tucker," and we would sing that over and over. After eating a big supper the chiefs told us boys to go and play, and we were joined by ten or twelve Indian boys and girls and played for a long time. The bucks and squaws sat around the fire and smoked and talked until about midnight.

In a few days a raiding party was sent out, and it fell to my lot to go with them as a warrior. There were about fifty Comanches in the band and about seventy-five Apaches, and for several evenings be-

THE BOY CAPTIVES

fore we started we would paint up and parade through the village, receiving the acclaim of the squaws and the advice of the chiefs. By having to go on this raid I did not get to see my brother Jeff again for a long time.

Our raiding party stayed together until we got aways down south. One day we discovered four or five men on horseback, and started after them, but they ran to a ranch and escaped us. Next day we found about twenty-five head of saddle horses and rounded them up, and divided them, the Apaches getting the most of them. We then separated, the Apaches going west toward New Mexico to see what they could find, while we went east. I think this was in the vicinity of what is now Big Spring, in Howard county. Here we found some cattle ranches and plenty of horses. There were about fifty Indians in our party, and we fearlessly went to the ranches and stole horses out of pens in the day time. The white people would dash into their houses whenever we appeared, and we would go boldly into the pens and get the horses. When we had about all we could drive we pulled for camp, which was about two hundred miles away. Some of the ranchers followed us, and although they were in sight of us several times they did not overtake us. We reached our camp ahead of the Apaches, but they came in several

THE BOY CAPTIVES

days later, bringing with them quite a lot of horses and three scalps, which looked to me like Mexican hair. Then a big parade and dance came off. I do believe there were over a thousand Indians participated in that parade. They rode six abreast, and I could not see the tail end of it. The Indians were singing, yelling and dancing, and their antics were amusing.

After the celebration the Apaches went north and we went towards Fort Sill, to the good buffalo range, and camped on Big Wolf Creek. Here in pulling the pack off of a mule I loosened the front girth, and the pack turned under the mule's belly, and true to his mule nature the animal at once registered his objection to such a happening by pitching and kicking and running about. I was laughing and holding the rope, and the chief was enjoying the fun too. There was a small keg of whiskey in the pack and the mule kicked the head of it in, seeing which the chief shouted excitedly, "Who! Whu! tudhug," which in our language means, "Damn that mule!" I let the mule go and the last I saw of him that day a portion of the pack was still hanging under his belly and he was still bucking vigorously. When I turned him loose an old squaw ran up and struck at me with a tomahawk. I managed to dodge the lick but a point of the tomahawk struck my upraised hand and cut a deep gash. I have the

THE BOY CAPTIVES

scar of this gash on my hand yet. The Indians bound up my hand, and it was sore for a long time. It was fortunate that she did not have any rattlesnake poison on the blade.

About two thousand Kickapoo Indians came and camped with us, and it was decided to send about a hundred and fifty bucks in to Fort Sill for ammunition and grub. But they would not allow me to go with them. They were gone about eighteen days and returned pretty well laden with supplies, which were distributed all over the camp, and nearly every Indian got something. They brought me two small cans of peaches and a bottle of cherry brandy. The bottle had whole cherries in it, and the Indians told me my father sent them to me. I knew this was a lie, and so I would not touch them, for I was afraid there might be poison in them.

After receiving these supplies we drifted on down south into what was called the Neutral Strip on No Man's land. We had not been there long when one day the spies came running into camp and said the rangers were coming. The big chief got on his horse and rode through the camp and exhorted the Indians not to run, but to make a stand and we would whip any bunch of rangers which came to our camp. He also rode to the Kickapoos' camp, and made the same talk.

THE BOY CAPTIVES

There was a great uproar in the camp when this news spread. Then about two thousand warriors, Comanches and Kickapoos, started out to meet the rangers, but I had to stay and herd the horses. Next day the warriors came back, saying they had seen about two hundred white men, but they ran away as soon as the Indians appeared, and they followed them for several miles but could not overtake them. They said these white men had the best horses. There were so many herds of buffalo in that region that it was difficult to distinguish them at a great distance from a body of men.

While here the Indian boys and I had great sport running down and catching wild turkeys, coyotes and antelopes. The antelope can run faster and longer than any animal on the plains.

I was not the only white boy in this camp. There were eighteen of us, whose ages were from 10 to 18 years. Some had been with the Indians for a long time, and some for only a short time.

Breaking camp, we moved on west and traveled for some time. The grass was high and wavy like an oat field just before it is ripe enough to cut, and even for one so young I was impressed with the beauty of the landscape. When we reached the Cimarron river we found it to be almost a wild paradise, and it looked

THE BOY CAPTIVES

as if there had never been a foot track in the beautiful soil. The sun was just setting, and as far as we could see down the river we could see antelope and buffalo grazing in bunches. The Indians killed all they wanted for supper. It has been over fifty years since I saw that grand sight, but I can remember it just as well as if it were but yesterday. We spent some time on the Cimarron, and the chief decided to send out a raiding band. After making preparations for the raid and when all was ready, the chief informed me that I would have to go along too, to help drive the horses back. About two hundred warriors started out on this raid, and we went south. It was the first part of the moon, so when we got down in Texas it was about full moon. When we reached the settled part of the country the warriors split up into small parties. The bunch I went with, after traveling for a day or two, discovered a man driving two good mules hitched to a wagon. They made me stay back with a few Indians while they waylaid and killed the man. During the attack the mules ran away and turned the wagon over, and dragged it for quite a distance, but the lines became entangled in a front wheel and brought them to a stop. By the time we reached there the man had been killed and the harness cut from the mules, and we led them away. The Indians stole about twelve head of horses

THE BOY CAPTIVES

further on, and we were driving them along, when we saw a boy going through the woods. They waylaid and captured him and killed his horse. He was about fourteen years old, and they made him help me drive the horses. When night came on we camped on a little creek and as the moon came up six Indians and myself went to a ranch to see if there were any horses there we could steal. As we approached the house we could see a lamp burning through a window. We passed near the house and went to the lot, but did not find any horses there. Just about this time some cows in the lot got scared at us and made a run, and out went the light in the house, and we knew our presence was suspected, so we ran back to our camp. We had nothing to eat that day, but next day the Indians killed a colt and just as they were cooking it they saw something which looked like men following us, and we ran off and left the meat on the fire. We traveled all day and part of the night, making two days and three nights we had nothing to eat, and the boy they had captured was almost starved. The Indians killed a cow, and began to cook the meat, but we began to eat before the meat was done. That boy cooked his meat pretty well, and we filled up like a dog. We felt better then, and headed for our camp. On the way we picked up about twenty-five horses. After riding day

THE BOY CAPTIVES

after day we found the trail of the main big camp and
followed it until we found the tribe. When we reached
the camp the squaws brutally beat the captive white
boy we had brought in. They made him fight, made
him ride wild horses, and tried to scare him to death
by shooting close to him, and to torture him they cut
off one of his toes. I felt sorry for him, but of course
could do nothing. This boy and I would be put on
herd together, and we always staked our night horses.
The boy got a good mule and staked him, and as he
was doing so the chief said, "Conchie, don't ever stake
a mule. They will pull up the stake and run off, then
you will be afoot." The boy nodded his head, but did
not understand a word the chief had said. There was
a lot of dried buffalo meat hanging on a lariat in camp,
and next morning it was discovered that the dried meat
was all gone, and also a buckskin sack, the boy and
the mule. They sent some Indians to follow him but
he successfully eluded them and was never heard from
again. The chief told me that if the boy started early
in the night he was fifty or sixty miles from our camp
when daylight came. The squaws wanted to whip me
because of the escape, but the chief would not let them.
They were sorry they did not kill the boy so they would
have saved the mule.

Other bands of the raiders began to come in, in

THE BOY CAPTIVES

small bunches, some bringing scalps and some brought horses, and we had a big celebration. One Indian brought in the scalp of a girl. The hair was over a foot long and black and wavy. They had had such good luck on this raid that they decided to make another, and they started again on the first new moon. I did not go with them on this raid. About one hundred squaws accompanied this party for a long journey. The main tribe decided to go over into New Mexico to see if they could find any Mexican traders. They had a lot of branded horses on hand and were anxious to get rid of them, and they could not take them to Fort Sill as the Americans would take them away from them, but the Indians could trade them to the Mexicans. After a long journey we came to an old deserted fort, somewhere in New Mexico or Arizona. There was no one to be seen there or any fresh tracks, and why it had been abandoned I do not know. There were some fine springs there, and the location for a fort was an ideal one. We spent about a week there, and the Indians killed lots of game in the mountains which surrounded this fort.

Two of our spies who had been out for some time, returned and announced that some Mexican traders would arrive soon, and in two or three days the chief galloped through camp saying the traders were com-

THE BOY CAPTIVES

ing, and they could be seen from the tops of the mountains. We ran up on the mountains and could see the Mexican caravan a long way off. There seemed to be 200 of them, all walking and driving their donkeys packed with all kinds of goods. The Mexicans reached our camp that night, and for about a week trading was lively. The Mexicans wanted to trade for all of the white boys and girls in the tribe, but the chief told them he would not trade the captives to the Mexicans but he would trade them to other Indian tribes. After the Mexicans left the Indians were well supplied so we drifted north again. The band which had gone off on a raid, returned to us with a few more horses and mules. They said they had had a little running fight with some immigrants, and the men let the horses and mules go to save their families and wagons. No one was killed in the fight. When they made the charge the horses and mules stampeded and they got them and pulled back for headquarters.

BODY LICE AND TERRAPINS

Body lice seem to thrive in an Indian village. The Indian, as a rule, did not seem to mind them, but rather gloried in being infested with the troublesome insects. Sometimes, however, they would become so numerous on the body that they would make unsuccessful attempts to get rid of them. When they catch a louse they kill it by cracking it with their teeth. When their buckskin cloth became "inhabited" they would hold the cloth over the fire and shake the lice into the flames. I have heard lice pop like popcorn when they fell into the fire. The bucks, in return for something I would do for them would agree to "burn out" my old buckskin cloth, or breech-clout, for me, and to get rid of those aggravating body lice I would often sing them "Old Dan Tucker" and dance for them. It was, as I have previously stated, the only song I knew, and sometimes they would ask me to sing some other song, but I would tell them that was the only song the Americans ever sang.

The Indians are very fond of dry land terrapins, or turtles, and when they found these testudos crawling about they lost no time in roasting them. One day Tosacowadi went out and brought in a great number of terrapins, as many as he could carry in a sack on his horse. While he was gone the squaws and I dug and gathered a lot of wild potatoes, a bushel or more. When the terrapins were brought into camp we built a big fire and threw the terrapins in alive, and we had great sport cooking them. They would get pretty lively in trying to get out of that fire. Being naturally a slow creature, it was really surprising to see how fast they

THE BOY CAPTIVES

could move when they got hot. We kept them engaged until they were all dead and cooked, and then we raked them out of the fire, cracked them open with our tomahawks, and with the roasted potatoes we had a feast.

We pulled west again, and after a few days travel we went into camp, and at a council meeting it was decided to send out another raiding party, and it was announced to the tribe by the big chief riding though the camp and telling us that he wanted to send out a band of warriors to get horses. I went along with this band to drive the horses they might steal. There was a large number of braves in this party, and as usual, when they reached the settled country they divided into small bunches, in order to more thoroughly comb the country, and at the same time keep their trail concealed as much as possible. After we separated we found a few horses and drifted them on. Soon we discovered some men following us, and gave them the Indian signal, but it was not answered and we knew our pursuers were white men. We rode at a fast gait, in a long swinging gallop, all morning, when we came to a deep creek and followed up it to where there were high bluffs on both sides. At the head of this canyon there was a fifteen-foot waterfall, and it looked to me as if we were caught in a trap, without any outlet ex-

THE BOY CAPTIVES

cept to go back the way we came and meet the pursuers. When the white men found that we had gone up into this canyon they stopped at the mouth of it, and sent runners back to the settlement for help while the others remained there to keep the Indians from escaping. When their reinforcements arrived, the white men left their horses at the mouth of the canyon and came on afoot, expecting to find us and kill every Indian. But when they got to the head of the canyon they were chagrined and disappointed to find no Indians there, and no sign of where the red men had gone out of that canyon, and it has always been a mystery to them how we managed to elude them. But it was done in this way; There was a hole, or cave, through the mountain at the head of this canyon, which was not easily found. The Indians knew about this cave and entered it. There were several caves there, known of course to the white men, but they did not penetrate the mountain very far, and after searching them out, they thought the Indians had been literally swallowed up. We entered that cave, taking our horses in there with us, and carefully obliterated every track and sign, and passed out on the other side onto a shelf and then made our way to the top of the mountain. Two of the spies went back to the top side of the bluff overlooking the canyon where the white men were

THE BOY CAPTIVES

searching for us, and saw the men had left their horses at the mouth of the canyon and had gone on foot up the canyon, and they hastened back and reported the fact to the band. We quickly saw there was a good chance to get some good horses and saddles, so we made our way down on that side of the mountain to the creek below the horses and made our way stealthily to where the horses were tied, and quietly and in a matter-of-fact way appropriated the animals to our own use. I think there were nine horses in the lot, and all had good saddles on them.

Now, in regard to that hole in the mountain through which we escaped; I am under the impression that this cave is somewhere in West Texas. I have been told that there is a mountain near Vance, Texas, which has a cave leading through it. Also there is a great cavern in Eastern New Mexico, called Carlsbad Cavern, which may have been the cave through which we passed.

So with the horses in our possession, we struck off in an easterly direction, and after going several miles we went into a big cedar brake to camp. Here we found a little water hole, with rock bottom, and we killed a fat horse, and roasted all of the meat we wanted. While here a signal smoke was sent up to try to locate other Indians of the original party, and the

THE BOY CAPTIVES

signal was answered about fifteen miles off east of us. After eating heartily we went on about eight miles and stopped, fixed a hole in the ground, and sent up the signal smoke again, and it was again answered, and we kept this up until we got together. The band we came up with had captured a little ten-year-old girl, and we had to get away from there as quickly as possible, for we all knew that our comrades were being followed. We turned north and traveled so rapidly that we were not overtaken. The little girl would get very tired, and an Indian would take her in his arms in front of him and carry her and she would go to sleep. They would carry her for miles that way. When we came to a big river we found signs that led us to the main camp, which we reached about sunrise. As we had been gone for many days the whole camp made a great to do over our safe return.

We drifted on to the plains country, and coming to a mot of trees, covering several acres of ground slightly elevated, and which could be seen for miles away, we found several springs boiling up out of the ground, and feeding a little creek. There was not a rock to be seen anywhere. We decided to make our camp here for awhile, for we knew the buffalo would come there to water. And come they did, by the thousands. One day our spies came in and said there must

THE BOY CAPTIVES

be white men in the country by the way the buffalo
were drifting west. The chief started out small bunches
of warriors to spy out the country for miles around
and find out what the trouble was. I went with one of
these small bands, in order to learn how to become a
spy. There were about twenty-five in our party, and
we went south for a day or two, and one night we
located a campfire, but did not know if it was a small
bunch of Indians camped there or white men. We
crept up rather close and waited until daylight. The
camp was in a small horseshoe bend, with small white
brush growing round it, and this brush kept us from
discerning who the strangers might be. It was planned
to make a charge and capture whatever or whoever it
was. So we were stationed all around, and when the
signal was given to close in, we dashed forward. Five
Indians were with me, and as we went ahead we came
upon a large dirt embankment. The camp belonged
to a party of buffalo hunters, eight in number, and
two Tonkaway Indians, who were guides for the white
men. A brisk fight opened up, and I am here to tell
you those hunters fought with coolness and determi-
nation, but they were all killed, except one, who when
he saw his comrades had fallen, threw down his gun
and held up his hands. The two Tonkaways ran out to
one side where the fight started, and were captured

THE BOY CAPTIVES

by our party, and with the white man, we started for our camp. Several of our party were killed in this fight, but I do not remember how many. Before going the Indians stripped the bodies of the dead men, and pillaged the camp of all it contained. The white man was placed on my horse and I had to ride behind him, but before we mounted the Indians disarmed me so the white man could not make an attempt to get my gun. The two Tonkaways were given a horse to ride and we went to camp. When we arrived there a great uproar took place, but the captive white man seemed cool and did not show any fear. The Indians resorted to many tricks to try and frighten him, but he would not scare worth a cent. They would run at him with spears and tomahawks as if they were going to kill him outright, but he would only smile. They made signs to him that they were going to shoot him, and loaded three guns with cartridges from which the lead had been removed and selected me and a white boy named Korn, and a Mexican boy to fire at him. When we pointed the guns at him he did not move, and when we pulled the trigger the powder blackened his face, but he only wiped the black off, and stood there fearlessly. The chief gave a yell and walked up to him and patted him on the back, saying, "Bravo!" The man, by his fearlessness, had won the admiration of

THE BOY CAPTIVES

his captors, his bonds were unloosened, and he was treated well as long as he stayed with the tribe. One night he stole a horse and escaped, and the chief let him go for his bravery.

The two Tonkaways, captured at the same time, begged me to get the chief to turn them loose. They asked me to tell the chief that they were only pilots for the buffalo hunters, and that they had families who needed them. But it seems that they had been acting as guides and spies for the rangers, and naturally the Indians resented this. But they did not want to kill them, because they were of the same blood, although of a different tribe and talked a different language. The Tonkaways were finally given a horse each and a gun to kill game with, and were allowed to depart with the understanding that they would never come back to kill the buffalo, or to bring buffalo hunters.

We began preparations for a long journey northward to get better range for our horses and hunt buffalo. We moved along slowly, across the country from river to river, until we got into Arizona, when we began to see other Indian signs, old camping places, etc. It turned out to be Hoto, or Blackfeet Indians, and they were on the warpath against the Comanches. They began stealing our horses, a few at a time, so the chief, To-si-ko-di, put us to guard the staked horses

THE BOY CAPTIVES

at night, I have often, while on guard, slipped off and went to sleep and when I would wake up I would go to camp and tell them my time was up. They would say "All right: send out another guard." One morning we got up and about twenty-five horses were gone, so the chief gave the alarm and called for about forty braves to take the trail. Myself and my pal, Moni-wof-tuck-wy, wanted to go too, so the chief armed us and let us accompany the band of trailers. We went out about five miles and circled the camp like a pack of wolf hounds hunting the trail of the stolen horses. One of the band found it and gave the warwhoop and we all got together and started in a rapid pace on the trail. It was then about 9 o'clock in the morning, and we traveled for about six hours, and came to where the Blackfeet had camped and eaten dinner at a little pot hole of water. We rushed on until about sundown when they were discovered a great distance off. Our horses being tired, we decided to camp for the night, without water or anything to eat. At daylight the next morning we mounted and started on and came to their camp where they had killed a horse and cooked part of it. The fire was still burning, and we jumped down and cooked some of the same horse meat which had been left, but had no water. We went on and soon overtook them. The brush was so dense we were quite

THE BOY CAPTIVES

close to them before they saw us, and To-i-von-ey, while in a dead run trying to provoke them to fight, called to me and Moni-wof-tuck-wy to stay behind as we might get shot if we ran them too close, but everything was on the run, getting faster and faster, and we did not have time to think of anything but keeping up. That region was covered with wild running roses, a shrub which would cover the ground for ten or twelve feet and take root again, and thus spread all around, and our horses often became entangled in these vines and would be thrown to the ground. Moni-wof-tuck-wy and I were in the rear of our bunch and riding to beat everything, when we discovered that one of the Blackfeet's horses had fallen and turned over with him, but the Indian jumped up and started on a run down a little creek. Our main party was soon out of sight, evidently not having noticed the Indian whose horse had fallen. We saw him crawl behind a berry bush, and when we rushed up to within about forty yards of where he was concealed, he began to shoot arrows at us. We raised our shields, with our left arms and then began to pepper that berry bush, although we could not see him. His arrows came so rapidly they sounded like sand hitting my shield. He soon stopped shooting at us, and confident that we had killed him, we ran to join the main bunch whom we could hear shoot-

ing and yelling some two miles away. We soon met
them returning to look for us. They had secured the
horses, but all of the enemy had escaped. When I
told the chief about the Indian we had engaged in battle
he asked me to take him to the spot and accompanied
by all of the rest of the band we went back and I
pointed out the berry bush to him. He laughed and
said he guessed we were just scared, and that we had
probably imagined we saw an Indian go behind the
bush. He insisted that we go up to the berry bush, but
I told him that Indian might be there, and alive, and I
did not want to take any chances. Some of the other
Indians then rode around the bush and called out that
the Blackfoot was there sure enough, and very dead,
and we all approached, and got down and looked at
him. His leg had been broken when his horse fell
with him. He had received three bullet wounds, so
we did not know if it was I or Moni-wof-tuck-wy who
killed him; possibly both of us did it. The dead Indian had a good bow and quiver. The quiver had about
thirty arrows in it. The bow was about five feet long,
and as I unstrung it the chief said I could keep it for
my own, but for me to give him my pistol.

We went on down the creek, looking for the
Indian's horse. I always felt a tinge of regret for helping to kill that poor savage with a broken leg, but of

THE BOY CAPTIVES

course at the time we did not know of his crippled condition. We got all of the stolen horses back and started for our camp, the Indians hurrahing Moni-wol-tuck-wy and I for killing a crippled Indian. I was glad to reach camp, for I was very tired and thirsty, and we did not enjoy the jesting of those Indians who were with us.

We drifted west for a few weeks and found plenty of game of all kinds. The Blackfeet kept stealing our horses and they got so bad we were afraid to go out hunting unless in good sized parties. Wild berries of all kinds were ripe, and we gathered quite a lot and dried them for winter use. One day one of the squaws and myself went over on a header or draw to gather berries. When we had secured about all we could carry we discovered a party of men approaching, and when the squaw gave the signal to those approaching they stopped, and did not seem to understand the signal. They gave no answer, so she came loping back to me and said it was Hotos, and we would have to get back to camp as quickly as possible. It was about six miles to our camp, and we had to go a somewhat round about way to get there, as we did not want to be the means of leading those Hotos to our headquarters. We made as quick time as possible under the circumstances. I was carrying the two sacks of ber-

THE BOY CAPTIVES

ries, but in our flight I dropped one. Soon the Hotos were close upon our track and we took a direct run then, and had not gone far before we heard a yell, and looking back, we saw them coming in a dead run. I dropped the other sack of berries, and began to whip my horse. The squaw ran alongside of me, and reaching over she took my bow and strung it on her stirrup, then handing it back to me told me to run and fight until we died or reached camp. On those Hotos came, and we thought they would catch up with us for sure. We came to a deep creek and dodged down into its canyon, and soon lost our pursuers. We concealed ourselves among the bushes and kept hid until all danger of being found was passed, then making sure the way was clear, we went on to the camp, where we related our thrilling escape from the Hotos, and securing fresh mounts, and accompanied by about fifty braves, we went back to see what had become of the enemy. They got our berries, and from signs we found, we knew they had gone back the way they came.

The chief and his warriors held a powwow, and it was decided to get out of that country, and it was agreed that we would leave the next morning. Accordingly, all of the horses were rounded up that evening and preparations were made for an early start the day following. But that night those rascally Hotos

THE BOY CAPTIVES

slipped in upon us and stole many of our horses. When they were discovered in our camp they had the horses on the run and dashed off before we could rally and fight them. Our camp was about three miles long. The spies gave the alarm from one end to the other, but it was too late to do any good. Most of our horses were gone with the enemy.

We started next morning, anyhow, and drifted on up the Monicho river. I call many of those rivers by the Indian name because I know no other for them. Monicho means White River. Our chief was afraid the enemy would follow us, and they did. About three days later the spies came in and reported that they had seen a great number of men or buffalo drifting up the river, but they were so far away they could not make out what they were, and they were afraid to get too close to them. The chief rode through our camp shouting orders for every boy from twelve years old up, and all squaws who did not have little babies to care for, to at once arm themselves and get ready for battle, so if they were called upon to fight they would be prepared. And he ordered all of the old men and squaws to pack up everything and start on south. While he was giving orders two more spies came in and reported that the objects seen were men on horse-back, but they could not tell if they were Americans

THE BOY CAPTIVES

or Indians. They said they had signaled them by sending up smoke, but had received no answer to the signal. The chief said we were in great danger, and things looked bad for us, but we would make the best of our situation. We were all called in companies, and the camp was ordered moved at once. All of the warriors armed with guns and pistols were placed in one company and those with bows and arrows were placed together. The country was brushy, with open flats, for miles. We got out and moved on down the river, keeping our spies ahead to watch for the enemy. In the open spaces we were drilled for about four hours, in order to be ready to meet the enemy. The manner of drilling may be interesting to the reader. The young boys were given especial attention. Our right stirrup was tied up to the girth, so that when we made a running dash to right we could hang under our horse's neck so they could not kill us, unless they first killed the horse. Every grown Indian had been trained to put his left arm under his horse's neck and hold the bow or pistol in his right, and shoot accurately on the run. We were trained to ride in battle in such a manner as to completely hide our bodies from view, and all you could see of the Indian as he was locked around his horse's neck was the top of his head and only one eye. If his horse was shot down he generally hit the

THE BOY CAPTIVES

ground on his feet and held his shield in front of him and shot out from under it. We were rigidly instructed to keep our bodies concealed as much as possible. We also received instructions as to how to charge and countercharge, retreat in order, circle the enemy, rescue our fallen comrades, and all other maneuvers incident to battle.

That night we camped and were not disturbed until about 2 o'clock in the morning, when our spies came in and said they had located the enemy in camp and had discovered they were Blackfeet Indians. Our chief called a council of his warriors and it was decided that we would not go and attack the enemy in camp, but would get ready and await an attack ourselves. We were placed in strategic positions and were given strict orders not to shoot at the approaching enemy until they opened fire on us, for our chief was afraid we might be overpowered, in which event the enemy would take cruel revenge.

We stayed in line of battle until late in the day, when we saw them coming. They formed for battle as they rode up on the prairie, and it looked to me as if there were ten thousand of the devils with their calico-colored horses and glistening weapons of warfare, ornamented shields. They were bedecked in their war-bonnets and presented a grand appear-

THE BOY CAPTIVES

ance, but I was too shaky for awhile to admire the scene. Our chief began to harrangue the warriors, telling us to fight until we fell, and to never give up. He said a brave man never lost a battle, and never got killed. All was excitement and expectancy. The enemy came up to within about six hundred yards of us, and made a great display of their prowess, challenging us to come on and fight them, but we quietly waited for them to attack us. But they did not attack. We faced each other there for two hours or more, when the enemy turned and left us, and marched back to the river without firing a shot. Our chief then gave orders for us to march to another point on the river, at the same time sending messengers to the main camp with instructions for them to keep moving while we remained to keep the Blackfeet back, for they seemed to want to fight, but were apparently afraid to start the battle. Those Indians claimed the hunting ground, and were evidently trying to scare us out. The chief decided it was best to get out rather than lose a lot of men, so next day we moved up the river, and the enemy followed us. We made another stand and tried to trap them by putting men down the river near the mouth of a little creek, forming a V. Our chief thought they would ride into the trap, and we were given orders if they did to cut them down from every side.

THE BOY CAPTIVES

When they marched in sight of us, they evidently suspected a trap, for they could not see our entire force, so they stopped for a long time, and after much discussion among themselves they turned back and rode slowly away. We waited until they were out of sight, then resumed our march and traveled until late that night, camping within ten miles of our squaws and children of the main body. We were out of provisions, and were afraid to go on to the main camp for fear our enemies were still following. We had no idea how many of the Blackfeet and Hotos there were, but we knew their force greatly outnumbered us. I had ridden and night-guarded and starved until I was desperate, and actually hoped the fight would take place.

We kept moving on and they kept following until we reached the mountains, and our chief was certain that we could waylay them there and whip them easily. When we reached the mountains we had to stay in camp for two days in order to give our headquarters camp time to get ahead. This was a large crowd of squaws, children and old men, and they had charge of a large number of horses. We expected the enemy to come on while we remained in the camp two days, but they did not appear, and then we went on and overtook our women and children three days later, almost starved. We had not taken time to kill a horse for

THE BOY CAPTIVES

meat, for we were kept busy drilling and preparing for the fight that never took place.

We rested up for a few days, and then resumed our moving through the mountains, and one day we ran into another large camp of the Hotos. Our chief called out his warriors and made ready to attack the camp. I did not want to go into that fight, so I went to my chief and putting my arms around his neck I said; "Potaw, I am begging you not to send me out this time, for I have a big boil on my neck and I can hardly ride. It pains me so much that I cannot sleep at night." He was smoking his pipe at the time, and taking it from his mouth he said "Boxicokeloc, you may have your wish. You can stay here with Monia." Monia was his twelve year old son. He then caught me in his arms and turning me across his lap he looked at the boil on my neck and called to a squaw to make a poultice of prickly pear and put on it. She hastened to do so, and as soon as that poultice was placed on the boil I felt soothing relief. Our warriors went out and had a big fight with the Hotos. About sixty squaws and babies were captured, and many of their warriors were killed. Our band got about a hundred and fifty of their horses and brought them back to our camp. They were all good horses, and many of them had been stolen from the white people just a short time

THE BOY CAPTIVES

before. We nursed our wounded, but some of them died, and others got well. We traveled on. The Blackfeet and Hotos got together and followed us. A powwow was held, and it was decided to release the captive squaws and babies and allow them to return to their people. Before doing so, however, the chief called up eight of us white boys, and asked us what the white people would do if they had captured a lot of women and children in battle. I raised to my feet and said, "Potaw, the white people would let them go." He filled his pipe with tobacco and cottonwood leaves, mixed it, lit it, and passed it around. We all began smoking and talking and laughing and the chief said it was best to put the captives on horses and supply them with dried meat and start them back to their people. So this was done, and they were told to tell their chiefs that we wanted to make peace with all Indians. A number of our warriors were fixed up, each had a black spot painted on his breast, and they accompanied the captives back to near their headquarters camp, and then left them to make their way in alone. The next day we packed up and started south. The chief gave me two of the horses we had captured, one of them was a little heavy set paint horse, and the other was a sorrel with long mane and tail, and I was very proud of them, for these were the first horses

THE BOY CAPTIVES

that I could say were mine. The chief often told me that when he died his son and I could have all of his horses. Sometimes I thought he would never die. I named the sorrel "Tu hud," which means all horse. The other was "Castchorn," which means buffalo get- ter. And when we got down south we got the buffalo, too.

Before we had proceeded very far on our journey we were followed by a band of Blackfeet and Hotos, and we had to guard our horses day and night. The chief gave orders for everyone who could shoot a gun to get ready and meet him about a mile out of camp. We left the squaws to guard the horses, and went out, the chief placing us in different companies and put us to drilling. Spies were sent back, and returning they reported that it was old Yohemohino, chief of the Blackfeet, with a large force. They moved on down Rock river, where we had a trap laid for them and they went right into it. The fight opened about 7 o'clock in the morning. I and several boys remained hidden until about noon, when the chief made a draw off. About 3 o'clock he put us to guarding a large gap in the mountains to keep them from running away. The battle was resumed and kept up the remainder of the day and part of the night. We stayed at the gap all night without any sleep or anything to eat. Next morn-

THE BOY CAPTIVES

ing the fight was resumed, and we could hear the sounds of battle all the forenoon. About 2 o'clock an Indian came running to where we were watching that gap and told us we had the enemy in a close place and the chief wanted all of us to come and make a finish of it and try to capture Yohomohino alive. We were glad to hear this, for we were almost starved, and we knew that would bring the fight to an end. For about two hours it was hard to tell which side was going to lose, until finally the big chief and his guards started to slip away down the creek, when Monia, our chief's twelve-year-old son cried out to us not to shoot the chief, but to give back and let him come on. Fifty of our warriors hid themselves among the rocks, and Yohomohino walked right up to within twenty-five steps of them, and almost before he and his guards realized it they were taken prisoners. The chief held up both hands in token of surrender.

He was a fine specimen of Indian manhood, and as brave a warrior as ever lived. We drove him and his guards down the creek, and the battle was over. Next day we took him to our camp and sent back for our wounded, and dead. It was my lot to go back to the scene of the battle, and such a sight met my gaze. Most of the dead and wounded had been picked up when I reached there, but some were still to be seen

THE BOY CAPTIVES

lying about here and there, and hundreds of bows and arrows and some guns lay scattered about. The stench from dead horses was beginning to ascend, and we hurried along our work as much as possible. Everything we gathered up on the battlefield was packed on mules and taken to our camp.

But we had the chief of many thousand warriors a captive in our camp, and we were happy. He could not speak a word of Comanche dialect, and we had to converse with him by signs. One of his guards could speak a little English. He told me he was an American and had been captured while a small boy. He was a fine looking man, with blue eyes and long curly black hair.

Our chief was shrewd enough to realize that he could enforce terms of peace now between the two tribes. He wanted peace badly, and had long hoped for the time when the tribes could sit in council together and smoke the big pipe, hunt together, and not steal from and kill each other. Now that he had the means for bringing about this state of peace, he was in no hurry to make it known.

We moved on and came to old Geronimo's hunting grounds, where we met up with him and his Apache warriors. Here I met my brother Jeff again, and when I found him I hugged and kissed him re-

THE BOY CAPTIVES

peatedly. The two tribes stayed in camp together for several days and Jeff and I and some Indian boys had a good time shooting, hunting, playing ball, running foot races and horse races. The chief wanted Jeff and I to talk to the prisoners, but Jeff could talk but little English and no Comanche. I think Jeff had forgotten who he was, but he had not forgotten me, and we clung closely together. When we moved on Geronimo went along with us. They discussed the matter of releasing the captives on condition that they make a treaty of peace, and the way the proposition was conveyed to the captive chief was through me and the guard who could talk a little English. One day two Indians were seen coming toward our camp with their quivers upside down and empty, which meant peace and friends. It was a Blackfoot and a Hoto, and they came to ask for the freedom of their chief. They were marched into camp and given a cordial welcome. One of them could speak Apache, and soon negotiations were under way. A great celebration then took place, the treaty was agreed to, and there was much rejoicing. Tom toms were beaten, and there was dancing and general revelry. A song of peace was sung, which went something like this; "Y0-he-no he-no hi-no, ma-wa ca-ha-ca seben mutche pi-hesta hi-yera quet, morviste, seben muste no-ma-wathte sustone sura-manowin, lala lo."

THE BOY CAPTIVES

Translated as follows; "O, the war was raging, and warriors you must go, for we have captured the Blackfeet and whipped the Hotos. Now let the big guns rattle as they will for we have captured the bravest chief that ever roamed these hills. He gave up his gun and bow; that is what we wanted him to do long ago. We will now unite together and whip the Americano as we go. Lo, la, la."

The Blackfoot chief and the warriors captured with him were given mounts and provisions and turned loose to go back to their tribe. After that they were friends to the Comanches and never molested us. The two tribes would often camp together and engage in hunts and sports.

With Geronimo's band of Apaches we traveled south together, the two bands making quite a body of Indians. Jeff and I were together a great deal. When we reached a certain range Geronimo and his band did not want to go further. They wanted to stay in the mountains, so the tribes separated again. Tasacowadi tried to buy Jeff from Geronimo, because I begged him to do so, and Geronimo promised the Comanches that if they would go and get him ten good guns that they would sell Jeff back to them.

I think we were somewhere in Colorado at this time, and we traveled on until we came to the heads

THE BOY CAPTIVES

of several big rivers, where the country was so inviting that we decided to remain there a while and make arrows and dress skins for clothing and moccasins. I remember how it rained most of the time we were there. Soon we learned of some Mexican traders approaching, the word being brought in by a Caraway spy. Our chief sent word for the Mexicans to come to our camp as we wanted to trade with them. I was out looking for horses, when I saw them coming, about seventy-five of them, driving burros with packs on their backs. All of the Mexicans were afoot. They camped that night not far from our camp, and our chief sent to them for a keg of whiskey, and they sent it right over. After supper the firery liquid was passed around in a tin cup. Up to that time I had never drank any whiskey and knew nothing about it. So when it came my turn to drink I poured about a half a cupful and proceeded to swallow it. Great guns! I thought I would never get my breath. The Indians all laughed at me, and seemed to take great delight in my discomfiture. Several of us went into a wigwam and sat down, and soon the whiskey was passed around again. I was determined to show them that I could drink it, so I swallowed it more slowly and with better grace. In just a little while it began to get pretty warm in the wigwam and everything said sounded funny to me;

THE BOY CAPTIVES

then everything seemed to be going round and round. They were all laughing at me, so I told them to clear a place and I would show them how the Americans danced, and I began to sing, "Old Dan Tucker Came Too Late for His Supper." They got me quieted down, and passed around the big pipe. When I got still everything was whirling around me. I got up and went over to the chief, threw my arms around his neck and tried to help him smoke the pipe, but the live coal of fire would not stay in the bowl. That is the last I knew of what took place. The squaws picked me up and put me on a buffalo robe and held me there until I was too drunk to get up. I was certainly stewed that night. Next morning I was still drunk, and awful sick. Tasacowadi's squaw wanted me to go with her to help bring in the horses, and as I went along it looked to me as if all the hills had been moved, and were still gradually moving. Everything seemed queer and out of place. From that day to this I have never liked whiskey. That spree was enough to last me a lifetime.

By the time I got sobered up the Mexican traders were gone. They left some ground corn, like grits, with the Indians, and some brass kettles to cook it in. Stakes were driven into the ground and a cross piece put in place to hold a kettle and we proceeded to cook

THE BOY CAPTIVES

that corn meal in boiling water. When done, we took it from the fire, and each fellow who had a horn spoon gathered around the kettle to eat. Those who did not have a spoon used the end of their rawhide breech-clout which still had the hair on it, but they did not mind that.

A white boy named Korn, who had been captured on the Llano near Junction some eight or nine years before, was about as mean an Indian as there was in the tribe at that time. I do not know much about him, only that he was afterwards restored to his people, and was pretty hard to civilize. His father owned a candy store in San Antonio a short time after I was brought back to my people. The Indians moved on down toward Texas and planned raids on the settlers and to steal horses. Several bands were sent out, in-cluded in one of which was myself and this Korn boy. We stayed together for about two weeks, traveling, and then separated into smaller bands and went in dif-ferent directions, but agreeing to meet at a certain place as we came back. In the band I was with there were about twenty-five warriors. On our way we saw sev-eral cowboys, but kept out of their way, for we wanted to steal horses only, and not kill any people as we went down the country. We kept going until we came to a big river. Late one evening we discovered a

THE BOY CAPTIVES

man driving a yoke of oxen and leading a good horse, so we laid down behind a little sand hill and watched him until he went into camp. That night two of our band slipped up and got his horse. When they came back with the horse they said the man never woke up. We did not go far from there to camp. We were pretty hungry, as we had not had anything to eat all day, so we asked the chief to let us kill a beef, as there were some cattle near where we camped. He said it would not do to shoot a gun, but we could kill it with arrows if we wanted to. So Cachoco (Korn boy) and I went out and tried to get close enough to shoot one, but could not. The moon was bright and the cattle were so wild we could not slip up on them. We decided to rope one, and accordingly took in after a good beef. I missed my first throw, but Cochoco caught her by one hind foot and held her while I jumped off my horse and ran up and stuck her behind the shoulder with my knife. She began to bellow, and I was afraid some white people might hear her, so I suggested to Cachoco that we leave her and go back to camp, but he would not consent to do it. She soon fell down and died, and we cut all of the meat we could carry back to camp. The chief had a fire built between two big rocks so it could not be seen very far off, and after cooking and eating all of that good meat we wanted,

THE BOY CAPTIVES

we laid down and slept for a few hours. After traveling for several days we came in sight of a little town in a long valley under the hills. I have often wondered what town this was. We watched it all day from our place of concealment among the hills, and decided to make a raid on it that night. Early in the night, when everything became quiet in the little town, we hid our horses and made our way on foot to stables there and let out several horses. Cachoco (Korn) was the boldest boy I ever knew. He would say to me, "Now go slow, and don't be afraid, and I will get the horses." There were a few lights still burning in the town, as we crept cautiously along, the Indians with us all of the time whispering to us not to go further. Cachoco went into the stables, cut the ropes and brought the horses out one by one, and we led them back to where we had left our horses and half of our men. One of the horses kept snorting and trying to run, because he was afraid of Indians. When daylight came we were fully thirty miles from that little town, and we went into a deep ravine where we found a big thicket, and there we stayed all day, part of us sleeping a few hours and taking turns about watching and grazing the horses. Late that evening we left the thicket and started across a large string of mountains, and went over into another settlement, where we found

THE BOY CAPTIVES

some ranch houses. Next morning we struck a creek and followed it until we came to a spring, near which was a house. Just below the spring we discovered some women washing clothes, and hanging them on bushes to dry. We stopped and watched them for awhile, and then turned and went back up the creek. We could have killed those helpless women easily, but we did not want any alarm given in the settlement. We went around them and got back into the creek again, where we found two good horses hobbled, and one had a bell on. We caught theses horses, cut off the hobbles and bell and threw them down, and left there. Further on we came suddenly upon a house, were we saw a team of mules hitched to a wagon. We were discovered about this time by some people there and they made a break for the house. We all gave the warwhoop, just to see how fast those people would run. The mules got scared and started to run, but hooked a wagon wheel against a tree, and the last we saw of them they were kicking and plunging and trying to pull up the tree. We had a big laugh. The house was an old log affair, with only one hole in it, and a big old slathery boy was running so fast he missed the hole and went half way around the house before he could stop and turn back and hit the hole. We were so close to the house I thought sure they would soon

THE BOY CAPTIVES

begin shooting at us, but they did not.

We went on from there and came upon two men quarrying rock, for a chimney I suppose. They tried to run and get away, but we overtook them and they were both killed with arrows. We hastened away from there and late that evening we saw a bunch of twenty horses, which we surrounded and drove them with us. Part of them were gentle and part were wild. We caught the gentle ones and killed two or three of the wild ones to eat, and let the others go. Cachoco helped to skin the horses and cut up the meat, while I and an Indian herded the horses. As soon as Cachoco could roast a chunk of the horse he called me to come around on that side and get a piece. I did so, and found it was a piece of the liver, and although it was only slightly cooked and the blood was running out of it, it tasted mighty good to me. We started our stolen herd of horses in a run toward our headquarters camp, some four hundred miles back, which we reached in about fourteen days. We had secured thirty head of good horses on our raid. We lost no time in making the return trip. Some days we would go without water, and some days without meat. When we would get meat we would have no water, and when we got water we would have no meat.

When we got back to camp with a good bunch of

THE BOY CAPTIVES

horses and without the loss of a man there was great rejoicing. Some of the Indians who had started out at the same time we did had returned, and some came in later.

We then went on east toward Fort Sill, and soon met up with thousands of Indians of all tribes, Apaches, Cheyennes, Kiowas, Comanches, Lipans, Kickapoos, etc. We came to the Twin Sisters mountains, surrounded by a somewhat level prairie country. At the foot of these mountains we found plenty of water and camped, and the next day some of the Indians went to Fort Sill, about fifty miles away, for supplies. The government was feeding the Indians and trying to tame them.

While we were there a few of us decided to climb to the top of the mountains. We had to go on foot as a horse could not get up there. We started early in the morning and did not get up there. We found a cap rock on top probably an acre square, and a split place in it about three feet wide across the top, and several thousand feet deep. We threw rocks down into that crevice and could hear them falling for a long time. On our way back to camp we killed several big rattle-snakes.

When the Indians who went to Fort Sill returned they brought with them a lot of hardtack, sugar, cof-

THE BOY CAPTIVES

fee, and guns and ammunition, and we went back to our old haunts.

In a short time the soldiers and buffalo hunters began to get numerous in that section, and we would frequently hear of the different tribes having big fights with them. So the big chiefs of the various tribes held a council and talked over the matter of giving up that part of the hunting grounds or fighting for it. Part of them wanted to give it up and go further north. They lingered along there, while other Indians went out in all parts of the country killing and stealing. Our chief was preaching to us that every Comanche from ten years old must fight or lose our hunting grounds, saying the palefaces would brand us and make us work like they had the buffalo soldiers (Negroes), and whip us. That inflamed us and we were determined to fight for our rights. We began a campaign of raiding that continued for some time, in which we killed many people, and stole hundreds of horses.

About this time great herds of cattle were being driven to Kansas from Texas ranges by the cattlemen, and it often happened that the Indians of the Comanche and Apache tribes would encounter these herds, kill the cowboys and drive off the cattle for their own use.

I have often been asked if the Indians ever made soup, and right here I will tell how it was made. The

THE BOY CAPTIVES

soup we had may not strike the fancy of the civilized people but I learned to like it and considered it a rare treat when the squaws prepared it for us. They would take the paunch of a buffalo and wash it out, and if they could find a big rattlesnake they would kill him before he was disturbed so as to prevent him from biting himself. Then they would cut off his head about twelve inches back and cut off the tail, taking the middle part and boil it until the flesh would drop off the bones. The meat, which is almost snow white, tastes very much like fish. They would put this snake meat inside the buffalo paunch, and together with some choice buffalo meat, wild onions, wild potatoes, and other wild vegetables, the name of which I have forgotten, to which had been added about two gallons of water, they would put all of it inside the paunch, and after tying up both ends, would put the paunch in a big kettle and boil it, all together. When done it would be as large as a bucket, and it would keep for a long time. Sometimes we would lay that paunch on the fire and it would swell and grow until it seemed ready to burst, when we would take it off and open it and then we would have hot soup ready to serve. And it was good. When the contents were all eaten, we would often gamble to see who would get the paunch, which itself was delicious.

THE BOY CAPTIVES

The chief ordered out a lot of warriors to go on a raid, so we painted up and made ready to start. The Korn boy, Cachoco, went this time, with a party of about 200 of us, down into Texas. It was at the time of the first new moon, and we felt confident that our raid would be successful. We traveled down Red River for many miles, and the first sign of white people we saw was a little camp fire a long way off. The chief called some of us to him and said he wanted several to slip up to the camp on foot and ascertain if it was an Indian encampment or white people, and if white people we were to see if they had any horses, but not to make any fight on the camp. I was so sleepy I could hardly sit on my horse, so I did not go with the party to that camp. Cachoco went, with several others, and when they returned they reported that it was a wagon, with a tent, and they found four horses, which they brought back with them. We did not disturb the camp, but went on our way leaving the campers to discover as best they could that they were left afoot. We traveled on for some distance and then camped until morning. Next day we went south and reached the Big Sandy. Afterwards we crossed the two Trinity rivers, and headed for the settlements. I know these last named rivers, because I have been there since I returned to civilization, and I showed some of my cow-

THE BOY CAPTIVES

boy friends where we camped and told them about what the Indians did on this trip, and they remembered the circumstances of that raid. Some of these same cowboys told me they were living down on the San Saba when this raid occurred and the reason the ranchmen did not follow us from there was because our number was estimated at 200, and we were considered too numerous for pursuit.

We reached the Concho river, and went up it for a ways, but not as far as Fort Concho, for we knew soldiers were stationed there, and it was our intention to avoid coming in contact with the troops. One day we came to a little lane which led to a cabin, and we saw a white man there. When we reached the house the man was not to be found. We secured four or five horses and mules here, and Cachoco went into the house, got fire out of the fireplace and set the house on fire, then went to a hay stack and set it on fire also.

We went on and some of the Indians came upon three women on the river, fishing I suppose, and they killed all three of them. When I reached there they were scalping these women. I learned after I was brought back that these women were named Honeywell, or Huniwell. We left that region and went into a sandy, postoak country, I think it must have been Brown county, and the Indians killed a whole

THE BOY CAPTIVES

family and took a little eight-year-old boy captive. We stole horses from every ranch we came to, and the chief made me and twelve Indian boys drive those horses on ahead. A bunch of men were discovered on our trail and we had to ride in a swinging gallop until night, when we camped and killed some horses to eat. We laid down and slept until about 2 a.m., when the moon came up, and we again set out, traveling the balance of the night. Next morning we were about twenty miles from there. The chief placed some blankets on his horse in front of him, and taking the little boy, he made him as comfortable as possible, and carried him in his arms seated on those blankets. The little fellow was much wearied and looked sick. They killed a cow and cut her bag open to get the milk for this boy.

When we reached Big Sandy the Indians ran onto a mail carrier and killed him. They took his horse and the mail bag and after going some distance they cut the mail bag open, and scattered the contents to the winds. They kept the leather pouch to use in making moccasin soles.

The Indians had tied a number of scalps to my saddle, and they began to stink and the hair began to come off. We had no time to dry them, so I told the chief I was going to throw them away, but he said

THE BOY CAPTIVES

"No." At dinner time he stretched those scalps on my shield to dry. He was keeping them for a big dance, to show what he had killed. My old chief, Tasacowadi, was not so hard hearted, and I was always glad to get back to him and my lepia (foster mother.) His son was almost a brother to me, too.

When we got back to our headquarters with our stolen horses, and the little boy captive, there was much rejoicing. But the first opportunity Tasacowadi found he sent the little boy captive to Fort Sill. I do not know how much ransom the Indians got for him. The lad had a large running sore on his legs from riding the old Indian saddles.

The United States government was getting tired of feeding the Indians and supplying them with guns and ammunition to fight with, so measures were taken toward putting a stop to the raids by sending troops to prevent them. At first the Indians were not afraid of these soldiers, and were inclined to treat the matter as a huge joke. They would overpower the ranchmen and steal their stock, kill settlers, and commit all kinds of outrages. But this was only the beginning of the end, for in due time the Indian had to give in to his superior, the white man.

One morning I got up to build the fire. It was just at good daylight. The camp was about two miles long

THE BOY CAPTIVES

and no one else in that whole village seemed astir. Suddenly I heard the roar of guns, and looking down toward the end of the village, I saw smoke rising. I called to my chief to get up quick, for something was happening in camp. He grabbed his gun and rushed out, followed by the squaws. He yelled to me that it was an attack by white men, and for us all to run. One squaw had a little baby. She picked it up and started for the creek. My old gray mule was staked nearby by the foot. The chief jumped on the mule, took his son up behind him, and then put out his foot and told me to climb on too, which I did in a great big hurry, and away we went. But in our haste we had forgotten to cut the stake rope, and down came the mule, throwing all three of us in a pile. The chief sprang to his feet, cut the rope and we all got on again and rode for dear life.

General McKenzie had slipped up on us during the night, with his troops, and waited until daylight to try and capture the whole camp. By the time we were mounted and ready to ride the fight was on in earnest, and at close quarters. That old gray mule was scared badly, and when the chief gave a yell and turned him loose he almost quit the earth. General McKenzie was leading the attack on one side of us, and a captain of rangers was leading the attack on the other side, while a whole string of soldiers were following us and literally pumping lead into our badly demoralized camp. We had to run about four hundred yards to escape from the fight, but about five hundred succeeded in getting away. They killed our horses so fast in front a good many fell over them. As we were running Cachoco's horse was shot down in front of us. He squatted down among the bushes and as General McKenzie passed by he put an arrow through his jacket, barely missing the skin. General McKenzie told me of this incident afterward, when I had a long talk with him at Fort Concho. Cachoco never ran. He shot all of his arrows away, but he left several dead men to show for his brave stand. Taken so unexpectedly the Indians had no equal chance, and many were killed. It seems that the soldiers tried to make a massacre of this attack, for they killed squaws, babies, warriors and old white headed men. The band of us who escaped went up the creek and circled around a little ridge and watched them fight. The chief sent runners to other Indian camps to ask for help, and by night our force had increased to fully one thousand warriors, and while we were getting ready to make a bold stand, the fight stopped, about 3 o'clock p.m. The troops captured all of our loose horses, several thousand, and moved down the creek about ten

THE BOY CAPTIVES

miles, and we returned to the scene of battle and picked up all of the wounded. This little creek was of running water with deep holes from fifty to seventy-five yards long. Long grass grew along the edges of the stream and hung over the water. Many of the Indians escaped by jumping into the water and hiding under the overhanging grass. So many were killed and wounded in the water that it was red from hole to hole with blood. The camp was wholly destroyed, and there were many dead soldiers and horses lying about.

The soldiers had captured many of the Indians and took them along with them, herding them like cattle. Among the captured was our second chief, a long, slim, red-looking Indian. He wore the black star painted on his breast indicating bravery. The captives were all afoot, and this Indian broke out of the herd and ran for a long distance before he was overtaken. His pursuers succeeded in roping him back to the herd, more dead than alive. General McKenzie also told me about this, as did the chief when he got away and came back to the tribe.

We fixed up to follow the soldiers and try to rescue our people as well as retake our horses. After what I had seen that day I was mad all over, and was willing to risk anything to get even with the soldiers.

THE BOY CAPTIVES

We had good horses and good arms, and although our chief told us he did not think we could whip the enemy, we were determined to have another battle and try to stampede the horses. We started on their trail, leaving the squaws behind to care for the wounded. I will never forget my horse; he was a big, long, slab-sided red roan, and a splendid traveler. We rode fast until we located the camp of the soldiers, then we halted and watched them until dark. They had a number of wagons which had been formed in a circle, in the center of which had been placed the captured Indians, and these were being guarded by a large force of soldiers, while other soldiers were herding the horses. We awaited until darkness had enveloped the earth, and then, guided only by starlight, we approached to within a hundred and fifty yards of the camp, to await the chief's signal for attack. When the signal was given it found us all ready to make the charge. With loud yells we dashed forward shooting at the guards, who promptly returned the fire. The Indians in the camp were quick to take advantage of the confusion, and many of them made their escape, but with fixed bayonets the guards held most of them in check. Some of the Indians crawled out between the wagon spokes, and some even crawled through the soldiers' legs in getting away. When I had fought

THE BOY CAPTIVES

for some time I discovered my gun was empty, so Old Roan and I left there. I could not hold my horse. The harder I pulled the faster he ran. The soldiers turned the captured horses loose to save their camp, and these were in a stampede, all seemed to be running for dear life. Soon I found myself right in the middle of the running horses. I managed to work my way to the outside of the herd and found that part of the Indians had followed up to recapture the horses. We went some distance and made camp about daylight, and all through the day Indians were straggling in from the scene of the night before. About two hundred succeeded in making their escape. General McKenzie told me afterwards that he succeeded in taking one hundred and fifty to Fort Concho, driving them like sheep; most of these were squaws and children.

A large band of the Indians followed McKenzie's troops toward Fort Concho, but returned and said they were not able to overtake them.

(NOTE - The fight above mentioned took place September 20th, 1872, at the mouth of McClellan's Creek, a fork of the North Fork of Red River, and was between a portion of the Fourth Calvary under General McKenzie and Mow-Wis' band of Comanches. A full account of the engagement is given in "Revellie

THE BOY CAPTIVES

and Taps," by Captain R. G. Carter, Retired, Army and Navy Club, Washington, D. C.)

The Indians were greatly distressed over their failure to rescue the captives, and every night for a long time I could hear the old squaws crying away out from camp, mourning for their dead. They would gash themselves with knives, and when they returned to camp their faces and arms and breasts showed signs of the mutilation which they underwent in their agony.

We left that region and went northwest, crossing rocky mountains, sand hills and dry plains, and reached hunting grounds where we were not bothered. Some of our wounded died, and we had to cut poles to make high scaffolds on which to place the dead bodies. These scaffolds were usually placed on some lonely high point. The dead warrior would be lashed on top of the scaffold, and all of his belongings placed beside him, his bow and quiver, shield, gun, and such other trinkets as he prized in life, and his horse or dog would be killed and left at the foot of the scaffold. This kind of a funeral always made me sad.

In this region we did not have to guard our horses, or send out spies to guard against a surprise attack. We were in a great measure safe from molestation, so we rested in camp, made arrows, dressed buckskin, and made moccasins, for winter time was coming on

THE BOY CAPTIVES

apace. It was here that I killed my first elk, near a little spring in the hills, where all kinds of game abounded. Four or five of us went to that little spring and camped overnight, so the elk could not come in to water at night, and would be compelled to come in the daytime. Moni-wof-tuck-wy and Cachoco dressed me up in a garb of green leaves and limbs and tied them on me so I would look like a green bush, and put me on the upper side from where the wind was blowing, to prevent the game from scenting me. They gave me their best gun, and told me to be careful, take good aim and be sure to make a dead shot. When they saw the elk approaching they ran and concealed themselves, and watched me get the game. Three of the elk came down to water, and when they got close to me I almost had "buck ague," and felt like running away. They looked so big. I was standing straight up and had a good bead on them. They came closer and closer, and I began to hold my breath and get weak in the knees. When they had approached to within about ten steps of me, I cracked down on the leader, a big fellow with a magnificent set of horns that resembled a bush top, and dropped him in his tracks. The other two turned and ran away. When we carried the meat into camp old Tasacowadi, my chief, was loud in his praise of my marksmanship and was very proud of

THE BOY CAPTIVES

my achievement.

On account of General McKenzie killing so many of our band, and taking others captive, a lot of the squaws who lost sons in that fight, had brooded a grudge against all of the white boys in the tribe, and had made threats that if they ever caught us out of camp they would kill us. My old foster mother, Limpia, the chief's wife, had told us of these threats and had warned us that if any squaw or buck came to us in the woods that we should be on our guard and not let them get too close, but to watch them always. Tasacowadi had given us arms and told us to tell them to keep away, but if they would not, for us to kill them if we could, for we were not to blame for what had been done. One day I was out about four miles from camp, driving our horses in for water, when I saw two men coming in my direction. I stopped and watched them, and at first thought they were white men, so I gave them the Indian sign but they did not answer it, and kept coming right on. Soon I saw they were Indians. They came running up to me, reeling from side to side, and when within a few feet they stopped and began chattering in a language I could not understand. They had a long cow's horn, fixed like a bottle, and both were beastly drunk. They wanted me to drink with them, and when I refused

THE BOY CAPTIVES

they began to whip my horse over the head with a rope. I thought it best to run away from them, so I lit out, with them after me. I was really afraid of them. They had probably traded for the whiskey from Mexicans, and were evidently bent on being sociable, but I did not take it that way. They followed me for some distance, whooping and yelling, and when I came to a little creek and tried to hide they stayed so close I could not get away from them. I got my horse down a steep embankment, and made up my mind that I would kill both of them if they came down that bank. They had nothing to shoot with, or perhaps they would have killed me. When they were trying to get their horses down the embankment I fired and killed one of the horses. I then galloped down the creek, waited awhile, and as they did not follow me, I went back to my herd and drove the horses to camp. When I told Tasacowadi what had happened he laughed and said, "I wish you had killed both of them and brought me the whiskey." We never heard any more of those two Kickapoos.

About this time a large band of Apaches came to our camp, and told us about Chief Geronimo having had a big fight with the rangers back in the mountains. They said he whipped the rangers, and I was uneasy for fear that Brother Jeff was killed in the fight,

THE BOY CAPTIVES

for he was with Geronimo. The big chiefs all got together and held a big powwow, at which it was decided to move over into Utah, in the Salt Lake country, and in a very short time we were on our way. There was a big tribe of Monehaw Indians in that region, and when we got there the Monehaws were on the warpath against the whites. The country was settling up, and the Indians were stealing the white people's horses. We camped about twenty miles distant from a little town, and a band of us was sent in to that town one night to see if we could steal a few horses there. Cachoco and I were in this party. It was all prairie land for miles and miles, and we came in sight of the town before night, so we had to wait for darkness before entering. We saw many big piles of dirt, and could not imagine what they were. Later we learned that these piles of dirt were dugouts which were used for houses. After dark we stealthily went into the little town, but did not see any horses or any place to keep horses. We could not tell whether we were in the middle of the town or not, for most of the houses were under ground. When we were convinced that there was nothing there for us we started back, and to have a little fun Cachoco fired off his gun and gave a yell. We started in a run, and as we raced along an Apache's horse fell into a dugout about ten feet deep. We could

THE BOY CAPTIVES

not get the horse out and had to leave him there. The white people in that country seemed to be poor and had no stock of any kind, so we moved out of there and went on south, I do not know just where, but I think it must have been down in Colorado. We camped on a big river, perhaps a north prong of the Arkansas. The chief ordered about five hundred to go out on a raid, and wanted me, Moni-wof-tuck-wy, Cachoco and Toi-von-ey to go along to help drive back the horses stolen. We all got ready, painted up in style, armed ourselves with guns, bows and arrows, tomahawks, shield, flint and steels for fire-making. We carried no bedding. If the nights were a little cool we would lay down and bunch up like hogs. We had a Kickapoo chief for a leader, and he would camp every night and take everything easy. It was understood that when we got into the settlements we would separate and come together again further on. Every time we divided I went with Cachoco's bunch, and we did not attack any ranch house, but we sure stole horses whenever opportunity offered. The last time we separated we had a hard time getting together again, for we could not find any suitable smoke wood with which to send up signals for the other members of the raiding party to see. We gathered up a lot of dry buffalo chips, and dug a hole about three feet deep into which we put

THE BOY CAPTIVES

the chips and then piled in dry grass, and set it afire.
When it caught good, a wet saddle blanket was placed
over it for a few minutes and then suddenly taken off,
and that smoke went up into the air fully one hundred
feet. When they did this the third time we saw another smoke signal ascending about fifteen miles
away. We came together and found the band driving
horses, mules and cattle. We had not eaten anything
for almost two days, but we traveled on until we came
to a water hole where there was plenty of mesquite
wood, so we went to killing cattle and building fires,
and cooking meat. While this was being done I had
to herd the horses. Our spies discovered a crowd of
rangers coming, but the chief did not hear them and
when the meat was done they all got a chunk and sent
me a big piece. They decided to lay a trap for the
men who were following us. The chief moved everything over into a deep canyon and sent two spies back
to watch, Cachoco being one of them. Then he sent
three more, and later he sent five, and he told Cachoco
and Twovanta that as they had the best horses they
could go and give the white men a dare, while the
other three stayed back, and the other five would be
still further back to form an ambush in the shape of a
V, and for them to run into it when the white men
followed. Cachoco and Twovante advanced and when

THE BOY CAPTIVES

near enough they dared the white men to come and fight them; as they came on a run the two turned and ran back, and the white men pursued them, some of them rushing headlong into the trap set. Fighting soon became general. When the fight started I was helping to hold the cattle but they stampeded and I had to let them go. We had fifty horses in the herd, and when they started to run too, I and an Indian headed them toward an embankment and checked them there. The white men, of which there was quite a large party, fought desperately, and took refuge in a rocky ravine, else all would have been killed. It was getting late, the sun was down, and the fight came to a close. The Indians succeeded in getting their horses and saddles, but the white men escaped on foot under cover of the darkness of the night, leaving twelve or fifteen of their comrades dead on the battlefield. At daybreak we went over the battleground, and found the dead men. Some of the Indians cut arms and legs from the bodies and hung them up in trees. We lost our herd of cattle, but held our horses and captured some more with good saddles, so we took the spoils of war and went on our way, feeling sure that we would soon be pursued by more white people. Next day we came upon a little bunch of white men, who, when they saw us, ran like scared wolves. There were about 400

THE BOY CAPTIVES

of us, and they were not afraid of anything. They vowed to kill every Sermana (American) they could get close enough to. I think they killed many white people, including women and children on this raid, but I do not know the number, as I had to stay with the horses. They would go to the ranches in small bunches and when they would come back to the main bunch I could see the smoke from burning houses, showing that they had been up to their usual devilment. I saw so many people killed that I became used to it, and looked upon it as a common thing of no more concern than the killing of a cow.

After a long journey, we reached the mountains where we had left our squaws, but they had moved on and we trailed them by signs they left behind. We overtook them about a hundred miles further on. When they saw us coming, about eight miles off, they came out to meet us. Some were happy and some were sad, for we had lost about twenty-five men in the fights we had engaged in. Preparations were made for a big celebration. Tasacowadi sent for the Caraways to come and join us. They barbecued a lot of meat and made coffee, and it was almost like a white man's barbecue. The cooking of the meat went on for two days. A pit was dug and in it was roasted buffalo heads, and horse heads, which were put in the

THE BOY CAPTIVES

CLINTON L. SMITH
At 16 Years

THE BOY CAPTIVES

pit and covered up, and then a big fire was built on top of it and kept burning all night.

After the big feast, a great war dance took place, the "music" being furnished by a whistle and drums, the Indians uttering all kinds of yelps and sounds, imitating the gobble of the turkey, the bleat of the antelope, the boo of the buffalo, the bellow of the bull, the growl of the bear, the scream of the panther, and the howl of the wolf, making a bedlam of noises that were hideous in the extreme. Following this they shot off guns, and whooped and yelled like demons. The dancers were bedecked in all sorts of garbs, adorned with red flannel ribbons, beads, earrings, and painted in gaudy colors. The leaders held tomahawks and shields and spears which were strung with paleface scalps, and would march around over camp, dancing and cavorting. The big event lasted two days, and at nighttime the sight was a weird one.

We did not tarry here but kept moving until one day our scouts came in and reported that there was a band of Mexicans or some kind of Indians camped on ahead quite a distance. The chief ordered everybody into camp, and called for a lot of warriors to go and ascertain if the strangers were enemies or friends. After traveling all day we camped that night within about a mile of the supposed enemy. Next morning

THE BOY CAPTIVES

when we showed ourselves there was much excitement among them and they began preparing for a fight, but when we gave the Indian sign on horseback they answered it on foot, and we rode into their camp peaceably. They were Indians from the Black Hills, and gave us welcome, inviting our whole camp to come and join them. We carried the word back to our chief, and in a few days the two tribes were encamped together on the same river. They were sure enough wild Indians, and almost black. They cared for nothing, only to kill and rob. They did not believe in capturing any white people or Mexicans. There were several hundred tents in their camp, and I noticed they had mostly mules and burros, and when questioned as to the reason they had no horses, they explained that horses could not climb the Black Hills region, whereas burros could. They informed us that there were no white settlers for many miles from there, and gave such glowing reports of the abundance of wild game to be found there our chief was persuaded to accompany them to that region. We camped at the foot of the Black Hills, and found old Geronimo camped there with a band of about two thousand warriors. And what was most pleasing to me, I found my brother Jeff there, but at first he did not know me. I ran up and kissed him, and began crying for joy. Jeff

THE BOY CAPTIVES

and I were allowed to play together and with Indian boys every day, and we had many happy moments. Finally the tribes all moved together into and across a steep and rocky range of mountains, beyond which we came to prairie country. Jeff was still with us, and I was glad. I begged Tasacowadi to trade for Jeff, and he promised to do so before the tribes separated. I told him I would put my two horses in the trade, also my quiver and fifty arrows. Tasacowadi teased me and asked if that was all I would give for my brother, and I told him I would also give my gun if he would promise not to send me away from camp any more. I told him Jeff and I could stay around and herd the horses. He told me to go and talk to Lepia, the squaw, and see what she had to say about the trade, so I went and carried up a lot of wood and water, and was extra good to her before I broached the subject that was nearest my heart, and asked her if the chief and I should trade for Brother Jeff, would she raise any objections. She laughed heartily and said if that trade was made she would have three boys, and that would just suit her fine, but Jeff could not talk her language. While I was talking to her with tears in my eyes she was making a string out of sinew for a six-foot bow. She put me off by saying that we would be camped with the Apaches for some time and she would make

THE BOY CAPTIVES

up her mind later, and let me know about it.

We went on east toward the line of New Mexico. One day one of the chiefs rode through camp and made a big talk in favor of sending all of the warriors on a big raid. He said if the Indians did not get busy and keep the white people whipped back they would certainly take the Indian's country away from them. Great preparations were made for several days, drilling the young bucks, and getting ready for the raid. We then struck out, about a thousand strong, and crossed New Mexico, and went on into the settlements and began to kill and steal everything we found. When we got to a big river, we began to split up into small bunches, and I was thrown into a band of about fifteen, with a Sioux Indian for a guide. He seemed to know all of that country well. We went into some large mountains, the tops of which were capped with snow, although it was summer time. One night we saw a little firelight, and some of the Indians ventured near it and soon we heard shooting. They killed one man there and another got away in the darkness. We went some distance and camped for the night. Next day we resumed our traveling and for four or five days we found nothing, but a little afterward we discovered four trappers in camp. We hid behind some bushes about a hundred yards away, and I held the chief's horse, while

THE BOY CAPTIVES

the others were tied to bushes. I watched them slip up on the camp. When they were within about twenty-five steps of the white men they were discovered and the trappers all jumped up to run for their guns, but the Indians cut them down, killing all four of the men. They robbed the camp of all of the guns and ammunition and such food as we could find there, including the carcass of a deer which was hanging in a tree. They loaded the deer on my horse, scalped the dead men, and we rode away in high glee. They also put the four scalps on my saddle, but I objected and said I would not carry them. The Sioux warrior became enraged and started to kill me, but Cachoco (the Korn boy) interfered and said he would kill the Sioux if he dared to touch me. Another Indian volunteered to carry the scalps and that settled the matter. Cachoco rode along with me, and told me he would not let the Sioux hurt me, but to be on the lookout. I told Cachoco that if he wanted me to I would kill that Sioux at night and we would go back to camp, but Cachoco said that would not do, as he was a splendid guide and knew the country so well we needed him.

We came to a somewhat open country and found several sheep camps, which we robbed, and killed two Mexicans who were riding donkeys herding sheep. Soon we discovered a large body of men on our trail,

THE BOY CAPTIVES

and we pulled for the breaks of the Rio Grande, somewhere in the Big Bend country, I think. We sure had
to ride to outrun our pursuers. We got into the breaks,
and stayed there several days, and after leaving there,
one evening we came near a little ranch and the scouts
reported having seen two men driving up some horses.
That night we slipped in to get those horses and found
them locked up in a picket pen. The Indians did not
know how to get the gate open so they sent me to try
to open it, but I did not know anything about the lock.
It was the first padlock I had ever seen. One of the
Indians happened to have a file which he used in making arrows, and he soon filed the chain, and we got
those horses and went on in a big hurry. About the
third day after leaving there we discovered a bunch
of white men who were pursuing us with a pack of
hounds. We outran them, but the dogs caught up with
us and were killed with arrows. We drove our horses
for a long time, trying to find our headquarters camp,
but we finally located it, and there was much rejoicing as we approached. This camp was located on the
Platte River in Nebraska, I think. I remember it was
as flat as a shingle and the banks were about eight feet
high. The stream was about a half mile wide and ran
slow and steady. One day a crowd of us were in swimming and some of us made a banter that we could swim

THE BOY CAPTIVES

across. There were some little islands in the middle where we could land and rest. I got a chunk of wood to float along on if I should give out, and made it across all right, but returning I got into a whirlpool and came near to drowning. Some of the Indians came to my assistance, but I managed to get out without their help. The chief said he had known that river for many years and I was the only boy who had ever succeeded in swimming it at that point.

We moved on up the Platte until we came to a fork going north, and we followed this prong until we came to the Blackfoot and Hotos country. These Indians were very friendly and had been so ever since we captured their chief. We went to their headquarters camp and their chief and our chief had a great powwow. He gave Tasacowadi a fine chief's rig all covered with feathers and beads, and a cap with buffalo horns on it. This outfit was worth several good horses and mules. My chief was about six feet tall and weighed about 200 pounds, and when he put on that headdress the feathers reached the ground. Our chief and his family were given a big feast of smoked bear hams, and all kinds of meats, fruits and wild potatoes. Being a member of the chief's family I was privileged to partake of this feast too.

In a few days we accompanied this tribe north,

THE BOY CAPTIVES

crossing a great divide, and there we found the rivers all running northwest. The Blackfeet chief said that if we would follow those rivers far enough they would empty into a vast body of water, which I think was the Pacific Ocean. He also said no white men had ever been in that country so far as he knew. There in those majestic mountains we dwelt in absolute security, and did not have to keep out spies and scouts to guard against the hated palefaces. That was a beautiful country. I noticed one freak of that region particularly. It was evidently caused by a glacier. The Indians said it had been a snow and ice slide, off of one of the high mountains, and it looked like it had come for miles and almost filled up a creek. We had great difficulty in getting around it for there were mountains on both sides. Here were boulders as large as a good sized house which had rolled down the mountain side, and big trees, some of them four feet in thickness, were broken off or torn up by the roots, all piled up and down for a great distance. We went on further northwest and found many wild ducks, geese and water turkeys, which had come in there to feed on a fruit which the Indians called lolaco.

After spending some time in that region we drifted south again, and the Blackfeet and Hotos separated from us, then we blundered on southwest until we

THE BOY CAPTIVES

came to a dry desert country, mostly open prairie with a few sand hills. Here we suffered for water and grass for our horses, and the sand storms greatly distressed us. Sometimes these storms were so fierce we would have to dismount and lay close to the ground. In crossing that desert many of our horses died from eating some kind of a weed. That was certainly a God-forsaken region, and I have often wondered if any white people ever went there later and attempted its reclamation. We were a long time getting out of that region. We found some small salt lakes in the hills, probably in Utah Territory, in the northern part. The water was salty and full of alkali, and we could not use it. We finally struck an Indian trail going southwest and followed it for many days, and came up with the band, a party of Sioux going to the northern part of Arizona. They told us of a place where the white people would let the wild Indians come in and trade with them and would not try to kill them. We accompanied this band of Sioux and when we came near the town Tasacowadi stopped and camped and would not go into the town. But a number of our warriors ventured in, and when they returned they brought back with them a few things.

We did not tarry long here, but taking the stars for our guide we traveled south, and came into a section

THE BOY CAPTIVES

occupied by the Neobrarars, who lived in little huts with grass roofs. Here we stayed awhile and had horse races and other sports with that tribe. While we were here the two tribes decided to send out a raiding party, and I was selected to go along, but I did not want to. I asked the chief to not send me, and the old black rascal said if I would kiss him I could stay in camp. Bless your soul, I smacked him in the mouth and hugged him, too. The raiding party was gone for some time, and when our warriors returned we resumed our journey south.

We observed that the buffalo were drifting more than usual, and suspected that something was wrong. Tasacowadi said the unusual movement was due to soldiers or buffalo hunters, and cautioned vigilance. It was not the time of year for the northward movement, and we felt much uneasiness. The scouts came into camp one day and reported that they had seen dust rising like smoke out on the prairie and they believed it was some troops of soldiers coming. Orders were at once given for all of the warriors to get ready for a fight. Horses were rounded up, and there was much confusion in camp for awhile. Everything was packed up and ready to move at a moment's notice. Tasacowadi was mounted, and told me to hand him his shield, but in the uproar I did not hear him, so he

THE BOY CAPTIVES

ran his horse up to me and whipped me with his rope. This was the first time he ever struck me a blow. Only about two hours elapsed from the time we received word of the soldiers' coming until we were fully packed and on the move. We traveled rapidly for about twenty miles and came to another Indian camp, and there we spent the night. Next day our warriors came in and said they had seen no soldiers. It was all a big scare.

We roamed around for some time, and finally found ourselves in the Rio Grande country. I think it was. As before stated, I cannot with any degree of certainty state where we were, for I did not know the geography of the country at that time, and of course paid but little attention to it. A band of about 100 of us struck out on a raid, and made a long trip of it. As usual we split up in small bunches. Our band ran onto a man, surrounded him, and shot his nose off. He was left for dead, but recovered and I afterwards learned that his name was Coston. Coming on to the Nueces and Frio regions our bunch killed two old people and then went northwest, stealing horses as we went. Crossing that rocky region some of our horses became so tenderfooted we had to leave them behind. A bunch of white men followed us and overtook us just after sunrise one morning, and we had a desperate fight

THE BOY CAPTIVES

with them. Those white men fought like demons, but we were too numerous for them and they had to run. They killed fourteen of our warriors and wounded many more. I was told after I came back from the Indians that this was a bunch of cowmen under the leadership of a Captain Jennings, and that he received an arrow wound in the fight. He is still living, and I saw him a few years ago at a reunion of the Old Trail Drivers at San Antonio.

I have been asked many times, "Did you ever kill anybody white while you were with the Indians?" When asked this question I always hang my head and do not reply. It pains me greatly when this question is asked, for it brings up memories of deeds which I was forced to do, taught to do by savages, whose chief delight was to kill and steal. It must be remembered that I was just a mere boy, and that I had, without choice, absorbed the customs and manners of a savage tribe. I was an Indian.

Leaving the scene of this last battle we went on and encountered seven white men who were in charge of a herd of cattle. We ran them off and got most of their cattle, which we drove off, and we were not followed. When we got over in the Indian Territory we met up with a large band of Kiowas and camped with them. We killed all of the cattle we wanted and traded

THE BOY CAPTIVES

the remainder to the Kiowas for horses. Leaving the Kiowas, we went on to rejoin our own tribe. On the way we met up with a band of Sioux, and the chief wanted to trade for me, but I told Tasakowadi that I would not stay with that tribe of Indians.

About this time word came to us that the government had decided to whip all of the Indians out, and one day our spies reported a large party of rangers advancing. We got ready to fight, and went out to meet them, Cachoco being in command of the band I was in. We had a desperate fight. I learned afterward that a Captain Rogers was the leader of the men. They had long-range guns, and my horse was killed. With my shield over my back I started to leave the fight, when an Indian told me to drop on the ground and hold the shield over me or I would be killed. I did so, and remained there for some little time, until an Indian came loping by with two horses belonging to the rangers, whose riders had been killed. He told me to mount one of them and run to camp and tell the chief to come and help them fight the rangers. I rode that ranger's horse for all he was worth, but before I got to camp I met the chief and a party of warriors coming on the run, so I turned around and came back to the battle with them. The engagement was fierce, the Indians using their usual tactics of battle, circling

THE BOY CAPTIVES

around, charging and retreating. Darkness came on and stopped the battle, and the next morning the rangers were gone.

We went north from there, and our raiding parties waylaid the trail herds and, while they did not generally attack the cowmen on the trail, they would under cover of darkness try to stampede their cattle or steal horses. This was kept up for some time, and then when reprisals were started our tribe moved back further away. It seemed as if all the tribes were on the warpath at the same time. The white soldiers and the rangers were invading the Indian country and fights were numerous. The different tribes worked and raided together, and they killed many settlers, burned houses, stole horses, and committed all kinds of depredations. If I should relate the details of all of the murders and massacres which I witnessed, and the raids I participated in it would require a book many times the size of this volume to contain my story. I will hasten on toward the end of my captivity.

Our band had moved further west and we were in the Territory of Arizona, I think. I know there were some mines there, but what kind I cannot say. We encountered some Navajos and traded horses with them. I remember the chief of that tribe had a pretty little girl, and he told me that if I ever got to be chief

THE BOY CAPTIVES

of the Comanches he would give her to me. The little girl was about thirteen or fourteen years old and quite friendly, but I did not want any Indian girl. These Indians were better dressed and looked more intelligent and proud than any Indians I had ever seen. We later met up with a band of Anadarkos, while some of us were returning from a raid, and they treated us with great hospitality, giving us bear meat to eat. While we were with this tribe I got lost from the bunch, and was alone in the mountains for several days, and came near perishing. Ravenous wolves, panthers and other wild beasts kept me in a state of constant alarm, but I was finally found by two Indians and taken back to the tribe. When I got back to my own tribe Tasacowadi rushed out to meet me and seemed greatly delighted over my return. They had hunted and hunted for me, and had given me up for dead.

One day some Tonkaway Indians from Texas came to our camp. They had a long talk with our chief, and urged him to take his tribe and go onto the reservation at Fort Sill. But Tasacowadi, while he treated them kindly, gave them to understand that he would not listen to their talk, and warned them to go back to where they came from. They wanted him to give up all of the white captives. After they left us we moved on and spent a great deal of time killing and drying

THE BOY CAPTIVES

buffalo meat. Another tribe of Indians joined us about this time, and some of the warriors went out on a raid. When they returned they brought in a great quantity of green corn which they had obtained somewhere. We had a great feast.

We discovered a big regiment of soldiers coming into that region so we prepared to move and to fight. We attacked these soldiers, who had thrown up breastworks for defense, and we had a big fight with them, in which Cachoco (the Korn boy) received a flesh wound in the arm. Many of our warriors were killed in that battle and many wounded. The fight lasted all day, and the soldiers withdrew with heavy loss. Our chief was satisfied to let them go, for the time being, but next day a lot of our warriors followed them. The palefaces never stopped, but kept right on, and when it began to rain and our horses began to give out, we turned back. When we got back to the battleground of the day before a most revolting sight greeted my eyes. The squaws had been there and cut the dead men all to pieces, and had propped them up against trees and shot the bodies full of arrows. I do not know how many white men were killed, but there were a great many, and a greater number of Indians, for the whites had the protection of their hastily thrown-up breast works. The squaws had stripped the clothing,

THE BOY CAPTIVES

caps and boots from the dead men.

We moved out of that region and went southeast, and some Mexican traders came to us. They told Tasacowadi that if our tribe would come on into Mexico and join the Mexicans we could easily whip Texas, but Tasacowadi was afraid to go in to Mexico. We drifted on and met up with many other Indians, some of whom had been to Fort Sill, and they brought word that if the Indians would release all of the white captives that the government would turn loose the Indian captives taken by General McKenzie and held at Fort Concho. Our chief left it up to the tribe, but could not get a one to say that they would do it. Some of these Indians mentioned above had brought guns and ammunition back from Fort Sill and Tasacowadi traded horses for some of the guns.

One night runners came to our camp and reported a bloody battle near the New Mexico line, and our help was needed. Accordingly all of our available warriors were made ready to go, and we immediately packed up and started. These runners were from Geronimo's camp, and led the way. The government troops had driven Geronimo and his followers back into the mountains and seemed afraid to follow him. As brother Jeff was with Geronimo I feared for his safety, and worried a great deal for fear he had been

THE BOY CAPTIVES

killed in that fight. When we got to Geronimo's camp I was delighted to find my brother safe. I renewed my pleading with Tasacowadi to buy Brother Jeff from Geronimo, or trade me to that old rascal so I could be with my brother, but he said Geronimo's band was so small they would all soon be killed and I would be killed too. Tasacowadi approached Geronimo on the subject and tried to trade for Jeff, but the old Apache would not give him up. After remaining with the Apaches for awhile we separated, and I did not see my brother any more until we had both been restored to our own people within the confines of civilization. Jeff was captured in Old Mexico after a battle with Geronimo's band, and my father paid a substantial reward for his return. All of this is mentioned in Brother Jeff's narrative, which is given further on in this book.

We moved up into Colorado, somewhere in the vicinity of Pueblo, I think, near the head of the Arkansas River, and found game plentiful. After spending some time there we went down into a region occupied by the Lipans, a fierce tribe, and somewhat related to the Apaches, and we tarried with them for quite a while. While we were in that country we gathered all kinds of paint, blue, red and black principally, to use in making up our war-paint. For green they

THE BOY CAPTIVES

used green coffee soaked in turkey or bird's eggs, only the whites being used. It makes a deep green, and taken inwardly is a deadly poison. They learned this from the Mexicans. I may also here say that soap was made from bear grass root, but the Indians did not use much soap. They kept clean without much washing. They made their arrows out of dogwood switches, and made their bows out of wild mulberry and bois d'arc. In slipping around through the white settlements the Indians would pick up all of the hoop iron they could find and would use this in making their arrow spikes. They also traded for this kind of iron from the Mexicans. Many people have asked me if we used stone arrow spikes. We knew nothing about this kind of an arrowhead, for they belonged to tribes of a former age. The Mexican traders also brought in iron or steel arrow spikes ready made, and all we had to do was to fit them on the dogwood shaft, and sharpen them. They used a kind of grass in making combs, or rather brushes, to comb their hair. And another thing which I will mention here: They would get me down, and with a pair of tweezers, pull out every hair they found growing on my face. It was very painful to me, but I had to bear it. Why they did this I never knew. They made the carriers for babies out of fine buckskin and two boards, providing long

THE BOY CAPTIVES

strings with which to lace them. Their saddles were made from juniper timber, and they made spurs out of the same kind of wood.

We rambled about from one section of the country to another, and while we were in camp in a certain region a small band of Indians came to us. I do not know what tribe they belonged to, but I remember hearing them tell our chief that there had not been much fighting of recent occurrence between the Indians and white people along the frontier, but that a chief named Round Tree had been bitten by a rattlesnake and died, and Manchac had taken his place as chief; also that the Caraways had been stealing white boys and girl captives from other Indians and taking them to Fort Sill and trading them to the white people there. We moved on and these Indians went along with us. We went north and struck up with a large camp of Cheyennes, and camped with them for some time, and while with them the boys of both tribes got into a scrap while at play that came near resulting in a free for all fight. The head men had a big powwow over it, and after smoking and talking the matter over it was decided to separate. We went up into Colorado and Montana and roved through all of that region, and while there met up with different tribes, among them the Sioux. Their Chief was named Cascon

THE BOY CAPTIVES

Memonton, which means Sitting Bull. We remained
with this tribe for a while and traveled with them. One
day we came to a place where Sitting Bull said he had
a big battle with some white people, and he showed
our chief the ground and how they fought, pointing
out piles of bones of some eighty of the men who had
been killed in the fight. There were still signs of the
desperate battle, broken guns, parts of saddles, cartridge shells and arrow points.

Leaving the Sioux we traveled west for a long time,
and one day our scouts brought in reports that we were
being followed by a great army. Our chief said we
could not whip such a large force, so we traveled day
after day until we got away from that army. We were
somewhere up in Wyoming, I think, and camped on a
stream the Indians called Yellow River. Here we
joined up with the Cheyennes, whose chief was named
Red Cloud, and later Gray Eagle with his Blackfeet
warriors joined us, and with a large force of warriors
of the three tribes we attacked a large body of troops
about daylight one morning, and fought them for several hours, killing many of them and losing many of
our warriors. Tasacowadi was wounded in this fight,
and his place was taken by another Comanche,
Enchiposato, (Black Bear). The bullet which struck
Tasacowadi deflected from his shield and entered his

THE BOY CAPTIVES

hip, and a short time later caused his death. This battle took place on Yellowstone River in Wyoming. The Indians' loss was heavy, and we had to withdraw.

I always claimed Tasacowadi as my father, and his squaws as my mothers. Now my father was dead, and I had three squaw mothers left. They buried my best friend on a high point of a mountain, upon a scaffold, wrapping his body in a red blanket, and placed his bow and quiver by his side, and left him there in that solitude. With a heavy heart and bowed head I followed the wailing squaws back to camp, until my grief became too great to silently bear when I, too, joined in the wailing.

We soon resumed our rambling, and in the course of time the various chiefs got together and agreed to quit fighting and go to Fort Sill or some other reservation and draw rations. The white boys and girls who were held captives by the Indians were being taken to Fort Sill and exchanged. They wanted me to go in too, but I would not consent to do so. They told me that my father was there and wanted me to come to him. I said, "No, no. My father was killed on Yellowstone River." Black Bear was now my chief, and he said if I did not want to go to the reservation he would not let them take me. He had several white captives. We moved about from range to range, but

THE BOY CAPTIVES

we had to always be watchful for there were Indians in the tribe who were bent on kidnaping us and sending us to Fort Sill. One day a Caraway came to our camp with a lot of fruit in cans and some peach brandy, which he said my father at Fort Sill had sent to me. He tried to get me to eat it, but I refused, saying I had no father, only Black Bear. After this Indian was gone Black Bear told me to always go armed and never let an Indian come near me while I was out herding horses. If any attempted to come to halt them, and if they did not halt to shoot them.

One morning as I was going out after our horses I saw two strange Indians coming toward me, and I gave them the sign and they stopped and answered it all right. I rode up near them and began talking to them. One was a Comanche and told me they had lost some horses. I told them I was looking for mine too, and they said they had seen eight of my horses over in the next valley, one of them being a spotted mare. They talked so friendly and really seemed to be hunting horses, so I felt no danger. We all three went riding off together in the direction they said they had seen the horses. Just as we crossed a little gully I found myself facing a big pistol in the hands of one of those Indians, who commanded me to put up my hands. When I did so the other Indian rode up and took my

THE BOY CAPTIVES

pistol away from me, threw a rope around my horse's neck, and struck off with me, a prisoner in their hands. They went over into the next valley where they had a horse staked, and making me dismount they turned Black Bear's horse loose and forced me to get on their horse, and we pulled out for a fifteen days' ride to Fort Sill.

We had a long hard trip. Water was scarce, and for three days and nights we traveled without a drop to drink. Finally we came to a little river, which had high banks, and we could not get down to the water. My captors knew of a crossing, and we reached there about dark, and saw a camp fire at the crossing. One of my companions crawled up near enough to see that the men in camp were rangers, and we had to go further down the river to make a crossing at a very deep place, which our horses had to swim.

As we traveled on from day to day we saw a great many Indian camps, but went around them, as the two Indians did not want them to know they had stolen me from Black Bear. Finally we came to some Caraways in camp. They had several white boys and girls to take in to the reservation. At night I was securely bound, but one night I got hold of an old file which the Indians had been using in making some spikes, and I managed to cut the buckskin strings which bound my

THE BOY CAPTIVES

legs, and got loose. I stealthily crawled around in the camp trying to steal a Winchester, but could not locate one. After a long time I located a quiver full of arrows, and one bow, and stole that. My next problem was to get a horse and be off, but I could not get one, so I left that camp afoot and traveled all night and a part of the next day. I was afraid to travel in the daytime for I was on a prairie and could be easily seen. I went into a small thicket of plum bushes and laid up all day. I discovered a party of Indians trying to trail me, but they failed to locate me, and passed some distance away.

I traveled for about a week, trying to locate Black Bear and the tribe, and I was almost perishing with hunger, but I kept bravely on. I discovered an Indian camp, and I determined to go there and stay with them until I saw an opportunity to steal a horse on which to pursue my journey. When I approached that camp several squaws came to meet me, and had lots of questions to ask, why I was out there afoot, and where I belonged, etc. I told them I was lost from old Chief Black Bear, and was trying to find him. I had seen some of these Indians before and they made me welcome in their camp, and I stayed with them for several days. They sent me and an Indian boy out one evening to look after the horses, and when we were

THE BOY CAPTIVES

quite a distance away I caught a good horse, one that belonged to the chief, and I sent the boy down on a little creek, telling him I would ride around a little hill and try to kill an antelope. The sun was just setting as I lost sight of that boy, and I rode away to find my way back to Black Bear. I traveled north, riding hard until midnight, and when the moon went down I lay down and slept until morning. I found a lot of prickly pear apples, on which I made my breakfast, and then resumed my journey. I traveled for several days, until I felt safe from those rascals who had tried to take me to the reservation. One evening I saw a camp fire, and waited until darkness had fallen to investigate, and when I came near I heard the sound of bells on horses, and I knew it was not an Indian camp. I drifted on north, and began to think I was lost. I came to a big river and I followed up its course for many miles. One night while I was camped on this river a herd of buffalo came down to water, and they got scared at my campfire and stampeded. My horse became frightened and made a run on his stake rope and broke it in two. So I lost my horse, and was again afoot. I had about thirty arrows left in my quiver. I traveled for many days afoot, keeping near the river. I found an old Indian trail and followed it until it got pretty fresh. The trail left the river and turned south

THE BOY CAPTIVES

and went out on the prairie. I was afraid to leave the river, so I turned back to the river, and it was fortunate that I did so for I soon found an old Indian pony that had been lost. I had no difficulty in catching him. I took off my breech-clout and hobbled that horse, for it was late in the evening, and I spent half of the night making a rope out of bear grass. Next morning I got on the horse and took that Indian trail out on the prairie and followed it two or three days. When I overtook them I found they were Kickapoos, and I went

C.L. SMITH AND WIFE, DIXIE

to them. They were greatly surprised when I rode into their camp on their pony. They began to talk to me but I could not understand their language. They

THE BOY CAPTIVES

knew I belonged to the Comanches for some of them had seen me in that tribe. Finally an old Indian buck came forward who could talk to me, and I told him the whole story, about the two Indians stealing me and had tried to take me to Fort Sill to turn me over to the white people. He told me Black Bear was away to the northwest and I had been traveling too far north and had struck a prong of the Platte river. They gave me some choice roasted buffalo tongue and made me comfortable. They invited me to stay with them, and I accepted the invitation gladly. These Indians went on South and one day we met up with the very same Indians who had stolen me a short time before. They took charge of me again, and told me they had a scheme which would be profitable to all of us. They would take me to Fort Sill, and exchange me for some of their brothers, and after their kin was released we would steal some horses from the whites and come back, and the Indians would make me a chief. That all sounded pretty good to me, and I thought it could be done easily, so I consented to go with them without further trouble.

These Indians rounded up nine of us white captives, one of whom was a sixteen-year-old girl who had a small baby, and we started for Fort Sill, about fifty bucks in front of us and equally as many behind

THE BOY CAPTIVES

us. When we reached the fort we stopped at a store and a man came out with a lot of candy for us. Some of the captives refused to take the candy, but I took what was offered me, although I threw it away later, for I was afraid it might be poison. The soldiers took charge of us and marched us to the guard house, where we were locked up. Soon they brought us some clothing, and a man with a large pair of sheep shears came out and cut off our long hair. Then they brought in a big tub of water and some bars of soap. We thought the soap was to be eaten and the water was for us to drink, but we soon learned that such was not the case, when a soldier took one of the little boys, removed his Indian rig, and put him in the water and began to scrub him. After we had all been washed we were dressed in good clothes and taken out of the guard house, put in a big U.S.A. wagon, and hauled out to an Indian school, about two miles from Fort Sill, where the Indian children were being educated. This school had a stone wall, about ten feet high, all around it. There were about three hundred children there when we were taken in, and the big gate was kept locked so we could not get out. Nice sanitary quarters were provided upstairs for the children there, but part of us stayed in one corner of the big yard the first night we were there. When the bell rang for supper we would

THE BOY CAPTIVES

not go in, so they brought food out to us in a tin pan.

We stayed at that school for four months. Relatives of some of the captives came and got them. The sixteen-year-old girl mentioned above was never claimed by her people. She was captured when quite young, and had forgotten her name. We soon became accustomed to the rules of the school, and when the dinner bell rang all of us would make a break for the table, get all we could carry in our hands, and then go outside and eat it. A Mrs. Butler was our teacher, and was very kind to us.

My father, hearing about captive white children being brought to Fort Sill, wrote the commanding officer there and asked that a picture of the Indian captives be sent him, thinking he could recognize me and Jeff in a picture, and would not have to travel so far to identify us. One day a man came down from the fort in a buggy, and the children and teachers began to crowd around him as he took a box-looking thing and set it up on three legs. It reminded us boys of an Indian burial platform out on the desert. The Korn boy, mentioned previously in this book remarked to me that somebody was dead and they were going to bury him right there in the yard. The man then spread a black cloth over the thing and stuck his head under it. We could not understand what they were

THE BOY CAPTIVES

talking about. At this time there were only seven of us captives left there, who had come from the wild tribes. The teachers took us by the hands and led us up in a row in front of that queer apparatus, while the man kept his head concealed under the black cloth. We began to get uneasy, and when the man turned the thing around and pointed it at us the Kahn boy gave a yell, and we scooted, and there was no more picture-taking that day. The photographer, for such he was, stayed around for a day or two, and finally succeeded in getting the pictures he wanted, and they were sent to San Antonio. Father recognized me and Mr. Korn partially identified his son.

I AM SENT HOME

Within a short time, all identification having been made satisfactorily, the Korn boy and I were sent to San Antonio under escort of a body of troops. When the Indians turned us over to the soldiers at Fort Sill, they did take everything away from us. I had a big silver ring, two brass bracelets, some moccasins with beaded work on them, a pretty quiver and six-foot bow, and about forty arrows. These things were kept at the fort while I was at the school, and when we started for Texas these things were given back to me, and it pleased me very much. This bow and quiver

THE BOY CAPTIVES

were the same ones I had stolen from the Caraways when I was trying to make my way back to Black Bear.

We were placed in a big wagon, and a brass band began playing, and we started for San Antonio, the school teachers and children waving us a farewell. None of us knew our right name, but we had been given to understand that we were going back to our own people. The first night we camped about fifteen miles south of Fort Sill, on the same creek Fort Sill is situated on. We could see the Wichita Mountains about twenty-five miles to the west. That night the Korn boy suggested to me that we steal away and go to those mountains. We did not know where the soldiers had placed our bows. They had us in an uncovered wagon, and a rope cable stretched out from tree to tree, and all of the big fine horses tied in a long row, each about six feet apart, and had fed these animals for the night. We quietly got out of the wagon, about midnight, and crawled to the shadow of the wagons and stayed there for a few minutes to see if the soldiers were asleep. The moon was shining brightly. Everything was quiet and still, the silence of the night being broken only by the stampeding of the horses. We slipped along the row and tried to untie two horses, but the knots of the rope were plaited over a snap hook, and we did not know how to spring

THE BOY CAPTIVES

the snap. We had no knife to cut the rope with, but finally the Korn boy thought of a big knife he had seen the cook using that evening, and had seen him put it in the mess box.

We went down the line of horses, determined to get the two at the end of the row, as we thought they could be taken out easy. When we came pretty close to the end we saw a man standing there with a big gun in his hand, and we both quickly squatted down. He must have seen us, for in a few minutes a bugle sounded, and every man in camp suddenly appeared with his gun in his hand. They closed in on us, and we made no attempt to get away. They came up to us, and caught both of us, and made a thorough search and took the big knife away from the Korn boy. Leading us down to the Major's tent they put us on a cot to stay for the balance of the night. Next morning we ate breakfast with the Major. I do not remember his name, but I have not forgotten that he had butter for breakfast, and we took it all out of the dish at once and ate it without bread. This seemed to amuse the Major, and he laughed heartily. He was very kind to us all of the way down, and gave us many good things to eat. The soldiers seemed to take great delight in picking at us, tormenting us in some way. We were closely guarded from there on, and were given no

THE BOY CAPTIVES

opportunity to escape. One exciting incident happened on the way which I will never forget. The grass was very high, and one day, while we were in camp the grass caught on fire. A sudden gust of wind scattered the fire all around, and in just a few minutes the flames were leaping eight to ten feet high. The fire had to be extinguished, or every man, horse and wagon would have been burned in a very little while. There was no way for us to run for the wind was driving it in all directions. The Korn boy and I climbed up on one of the wagons and watched the soldiers fight the fire with blankets, coats, wagon sheets, and sacks. They piled up in that fire four or five feet deep and literally smothered it out. It burned off about an acre before it was extinguished, and the danger was past. Several of the soldiers were severely burned, some of them had their whiskers and hair all burned off. The Korn boy thought it was great fun to see the soldiers in that condition.

When we reached Fort Concho we camped below the post on the river for a few days, and the soldiers fished and hunted some. There I saw the largest catfish caught in the Concho I have ever seen. Two soldiers brought it into camp on a pole between them. It must have been all of five feet long and weighed over 100 pounds.

THE BOY CAPTIVES

Here a distressing accident occurred, when some of the soldiers from the post came out to give their horses exercise. One of the horses ran away with the rider and came towards the Korn boy, myself and a guard, who were down on the river bank. The horse stepped in a hole and fell, turning a complete somersault, crushing the rider. We ran and picked him up. His tongue was bitten off, and his chest was crushed in. I was holding him, while the guard was fanning him, and he died in my arms before any of the other soldiers could get there. They put him on a blanket and carried him to the fort.

We were invited up to the post to see the Indians, about 125, whom General McKenzie had captured some time before. The captives were kept in a rock pen, which was still standing a few years ago. We found the pen well guarded by soldiers, and when we entered many of the squaws came running to us and grabbed us around the neck. We knew all of them for we had spent several years in their tribe. We were allowed to visit these captives as long as we remained at Fort Concho, and General McKenzie treated us very kindly while we were there. He asked me a great many questions about the Indians, but I pretended that I did not know much about them. He was trying to find out all about the Indians, how many were left in

THE BOY CAPTIVES

the hostile country, and where they were likely to be found, so he would know how many men to take with him on his next expedition. Here I will relate an amusing incident that happened one day while we were there on a visit to General McKenzie. The General had a pet buffalo calf, and this calf, strange as it may seem, came into his office. When the Korn boy saw that calf he made for it and caught hold of its tail. The calf ran out, we following. The guard yelled stop, but I thought he was saying, "stay with it," and I ran up and caught it by the ear. The calf bellowed and pitched, but we held on to it, while General McKenzie, who had followed us out to the yard, laughed heartily. The guard finally made us turn it loose.

While at Fort Concho we made another unsuccessful attempt to get away, but were apprehended after we had gone some distance up the river, and after that we were guarded more closely day and night.

We resumed our journey toward San Antonio. I remember when we reached Fredericksburg. We found it to be a town with only one long street. We stopped at a store where the soldiers were getting some supplies, when the people of the town, hearing that they had two boys who had been captured by the Indians at Dripping Springs, came flocking around to see us. They crowded around us so closely that the

THE BOY CAPTIVES

Major gave the Korn boy an axe and told him to give the Indian warwhoop and start at them, which he did, and the crowd dispersed very suddenly. From Fredericksburg we went to Boerne, and from there to Leon Springs, and camped that night under some big liveoak trees which were full of long moss. Along in the night the Korn boy and I stealthily climbed up in a tree and hid ourselves among the moss. The soldiers missed us and began a search. Mr. Aue, who kept a store there at the time, brought a lantern and assisted in the search. They soon located us in the tree and made us come down.

The next day we reached San Antonio. The news of our coming had preceded us, and many people were there to meet us when we arrived. We were taken to the home of the Korn boy's parents. Mr. and Mrs. Korn both cried, and hugged and kissed their boy, but he manifested great indifference to their caresses. He looked wild and stubborn, and sat down on the bed. My father and Mr. Korn were both well known in San Antonio. The Korns were Germans and owned the finest candy shop in that town. Mrs. Korn fixed us up a good meal, which I very much enjoyed, and after we had eaten Mr. Korn took us to his candy store and gave us all of the candy we could eat. One of the soldiers brought all of our Indian property to us at

THE BOY CAPTIVES

Mr. Korn's house, and naturally everybody wanted to see them, and it was here these things were stolen from me.

My brother-in-law, Mr. Coker came and took me home with him. He lived nine miles out, on the Salado river, and there I found my sister, Caroline. I had been with the wild Indians so long that I was a bit timid at first, but her fond caresses and manifestations of great joy soon made me realize that I was really and truly among my own people at last. My father soon heard of our arrival, and came to see if it was his lost boys. I saw him coming, and knew him instantly. Of course he hugged me and kissed me, but he went outside and around the house in a little while, and gave way to his feelings. He shed tears over his joy at finding me, but that joy was mingled with bitter grief because Jeff was not with me.

Next day we went home to father's ranch, about seventeen miles away, and there I found my other sisters and brothers, and my stepmother, and it was a happy reunion, which no words of mine can describe.

The Korn boy was absolutely uncontrollable. He kept committing offenses in San Antonio, until finally the officers there told Mr. Korn that he would have to do something with the young rascal. I was in San Antonio some time later, and he wanted me to run off

THE BOY CAPTIVES

with him and go back to the Indians, but I told him I was satisfied and happy among my own people, and would not leave them. Finally Mr. Korn put the boy out in the country on a ranch, but he stole a horse and saddle and went back to the Indians. He was sixteen years old and had lived with the Indians eight years.

I was with the wild Indians four years and nine months, and when I reached home my brother, Jeff was still in captivity. My father offered a large reward for the return of both of us, and still had hopes that Jeff would be restored to him. One day a letter came saying that a boy had been captured from the Indians in Mexico, and was thought to be brother Jeff, and that they were holding him for the reward offered. But Father did not know whether or not it was his boy, so he began negotiations which resulted in Jeff being brought home.

JEFF SMITH'S STORY OF CAPTIVITY

My name is Jefferson Smith. I was captured by the Comanche Indians at the same time my brother, Clinton Lafayette Smith, was taken captive, in 1871. He has related the details of our capture in the preceding pages of this book, and I will tell only of my personal experience while in the hands of the Apaches. When the Indians captured us they took us to their

THE BOY CAPTIVES

encampment far to the northwest, many miles beyond the confines of civilization, and there I was sold to old Geronimo, the Apache chief. I do not remember the terms of the trade whereby I became the menial of Geronimo. But several horses figured in the deal, and possibly a blanket or two. When I was turned over to the Apaches they branded me with a red hot iron after the manner of branding a horse or a cow, so that if I ever escaped or was stolen by other Indians they could easily identify me. I was then given the Apache name of Catchowitch, which in our language means "horse tail." When Geronimo took me to his squaw, she very tenderly (for an Indian) washed my face, combed my hair with a bear-grass comb, and gave me a buckskin jacket and a fox-skin cap, the tail of which hung down my back; also a new breech-clout and a nicely beaded belt, buckskin moccasins, and thought she had dressed me up in style. Then she painted my face red, with blue stripes up and down my forehead, and made a great deal of fuss over me but I could not understand her talk. The Apaches gave me plenty to eat, which was more that the Comanches had done, and I began to feel proud of the trade. The next day the old squaw and one of the bucks held me down across his lap, the squaw holding my feet and I

THE BOY CAPTIVES

thought they were going to kill me. They stuck large mesquite thorns through my ears, and left them sticking there. I yelled and kicked and tried to get loose, but to no avail, for they held me fast. Then they showed me why they were treating me in this manner. They were making holes in my ears for big brass

H. M. SMITH,
Father of the Smith Boys

earrings. They compelled me to leave the thorns sticking in my ears until they got well, and then they were taken out and left holes there. I can still wear earrings, even to this day.

THE BOY CAPTIVES

I was given a bow and arrows and taught how to use them, and I mingled freely with the children of the tribe, but was made to carry water and wood, and help herd the horses, help grain all kinds of skins, cut switches for arrows, go on buffalo hunts to help carry in the meat, ride horses in races, and make myself generally useful. The tribe moved over into the Rocky Mountains, where they met up with other tribes, and would camp with them to run horse races and engage in other Indian sports. They would make us boys fight each other, and seemed to consider it great sport. For a long time I could not understand their language, but I began to learn under their method of instruction.

When a buck or squaw would tell me to do a certain thing, and I could not understand what was wanted, they would get me by the ear and pull it hard and then point toward whatever it was they wanted. The Rocky Mountain region was a hard looking country, but it offered a safe retreat to the Indians, who would send out raiding parties to steal horses and murder white people, and then come back to that wild region, sometimes bringing with them captive boys and girls, mostly Mexicans. They seemed to like Mexican captives, because when they brought them

THE BOY CAPTIVES

in they could raise them up and no one could tell them from full blood Indians. We went into a region where there was considerable pine timber, and there we found lots of bear and other large game. I remember on one occasion they took me bear hunting with them. They saw two big bears and four cubs some distance away, so they sent me around them while they concealed themselves behind some trees, and when the bear caught sight of me they would run toward them and be easily killed. When I got on the other side of the bear they raised up and began to sniff the air, then they turned and went walking off toward the spot where the Indians were concealed. When they approached near enough the Indians fired on them and killed two of them, and the others turned back and came running toward me, the Indians still firing at them. The bear came near running over me, and I had to lay down behind a big rock to keep from being shot by the Indians. Right there I made up my mind that the next time they wanted any bears turned their way they could go around them themselves. The carcasses of the bear were taken to camp, and the grease was rendered from the fat for greasing ropes, etc., and the meat was eaten. The Indians killed a great many bear while we were in those mountains.

We found there also many mountain sheep, and I

THE BOY CAPTIVES

had the good fortune to kill a splendid buck, my first, while there. My Indian playmates were named Neiflint, Leite and Oblite, and they were very good to me.

In these mountains we dwelt in fancied security, until the government began to send soldiers in there to fight the Indians. I remember one morning we had just packed up to start for the Blue Ridges, which I think was up on the east line of Utah, when one of our spies came in and told us there was a great army of men following us. We then turned back to the Rocky Mountains, while about five hundred warriors stayed in the rear to keep the soldiers from catching the women and children. Those soldiers followed us for more than a week, but we outdistanced them and got back into the Rocky Mountain fastnesses where they could not reach us in the winter time. Only small armies could penetrate that wilderness, and the Indians could easily keep them back. Sometimes the Apaches and Comanches would get together and they could go almost anywhere, and drive back the American and Mexican soldiers who attacked them. The Comanches and Sioux tribes were strong allies, and their chiefs, Sitting Bull and Tasacowadi were brave and daring leaders, while Geronimo, of the Apaches, was equally as brave. Tasacowadi was chief of the

THE BOY CAPTIVES

band who held my brother, Clint, captive. Sitting Bull was the chief who staged the Custer massacre after I was brought home from captivity. I knew this noted chief well.

After a time we moved from our location and went to another region, and there we found Tasacowdi's band of Comanches. Brother Clint was with this band, but I did not know it, until I went to a spring to get a keg of water. He was there getting water also, and recognized me as soon as he laid eyes on me. We were delighted to get together again, for it had been more than a year since we had seen each other. The two tribes remained camped together for quite awhile and sent out raiding parties. Brother Clint went with one of these raids to help take care of the horses that were stolen. They started on new moon and were gone all of one moon. When they returned they had a lot of new horses, and some human scalps. Then a big war dance was engaged in. The scalps were placed on spears and held up where all could see them, and the warriors danced about. A large band of soldiers had followed the Indians back from this raid, and while the big war dance was in progress they slipped up and made an attack on us, being almost in camp before they were discovered. It was late in the evening when the fight started. The warriors hastily got to-

THE BOY CAPTIVES

gether to repel the attack, while the squaws and children rounded up the horses and hastily packed the camp equipage to move out of reach of the battle. The warriors rallied and held the attacking party until the women and children could escape. The fighting was desperate, and many warriors were killed. Nightfall came and under the cover of darkness we fled; we traveled all night, and our warriors did not succeed in overtaking us until after sunrise the next morning, after we had covered fully twenty-five miles. We left that part of the country, and traveled with the Comanches for a season. I was glad of this for I could be with my brother Clint occasionally.

These Indians treated me in about the same manner they treated Clint, as described in his narrative. They would tie me on the back of a colt or a wild horse and seemed to take great delight in making the animal pitch. After I learned to speak the Apache language and could understand everything I was pretty well satisfied living with them, and entered into all of their sports with as much delight as they manifested themselves. I remember a rare sport we had one time, when the Indians hemmed some antelope in a cove and roped them. They caught a large buck with the others and put me on his back. In these days of rodeos and wild west shows there is no performance

THE BOY CAPTIVES

that can compare to the show I provided on that occasion. That antelope buck, being quick and active, gave about four jumps inside of the space of a split second and threw me heavily against the ground. The Indians all laughed heartily, but I did not join in the merriment, for I felt like I had been "busted" wide open. They held the animal secure with a long rope, and put me on his back time and again, and every time he would throw me. He was fat and sleek, and I could not stay on. The last time I locked my arms around the buck's neck and its quick jumping slid me over his head. One of its horns caught in my belt and the brute pawed me fearfully before I could get loose. One old squaw in the party screamed and laughed with great delight at my discomfiture and urged the Indians to put me on time after time. I made up my mind right there to get even with that squaw the very first opportunity I had. She had a good saddle and was a fearless rider, and would ride any kind of bronc. Some time after this antelope episode I got a chance to cut almost in two a strap on her saddle, up under the leather where it would not be noticed. Well, it was not long until she was going to ride a wild mule. She saddled up the mule, put on her forked stick spurs, and got her buffalo-neck quirt, and prepared to mount. I was almost dancing with delight in anticipation of

THE BOY CAPTIVES

what was going to happen. An Indian held the mule by one ear while she got on him, and when all was in readiness the animal was released. About the third jump I could see daylight between her and the mule, and then I saw her, saddle and all, leave that mule and go sailing to one side. The Indians ran and picked her up, but she was unhurt. Then they examined the saddle and found where the strap was broken, but they never knew it had been cut.

The region we were in at this time was often visited by severe storms and cyclones. One day we noticed a big black cloud rising in the northwest, and the Indians began to put up guide poles on their tents, and tie them down with ropes and stake pins, and prepare for the storm. It soon came. It struck the village like a whirlwind, accompanied by rain and hail. Not a wigwam or tepee was left standing. I went into a fire hole and put an empty kettle over my head to protect myself from the heavy hail. Most of the Indians laid down on the ground and held to small bushes to keep from being blown away. Fortunately for us, no one was killed, but every tent had to be put up again, that is every tent that could be found.

The chiefs got together and held a council a short time after this storm and decided to send a raiding band down into Texas to steal horses from the white

THE BOY CAPTIVES

settlers, and next day about eight hundred warriors were called out. Brother Clint was in the bunch, all painted up and rigged out with buffalo horns, and went with the raiders. That was the last I saw of Clint for a long time. I thought he was killed, for I knew they took him along to drive the horses. They were gone a long time, and before they returned Geronimo's band separated from the Comanches and went further west. I was distressed and worried about my brother. I know he could have escaped on two different occasions, but he refused to do so because he did not want to leave me. He was certainly a self-sacrificing brother, and in many ways showed his affection for me.

The Apache warriors who accompanied the raiding band finally returned and found us, the Comanches in the band having gone to their tribe, taking Brother Clint with them. They brought a lot of Spanish horses with them, and also a little Mexican girl captive, about eleven years old. They could not, or would not, tell me anything about Brother Clint, only saying the last time they saw him he was leading the pack horses, four tied together. The Indians had a way of leading several horses at the same time by tying one horse to the tail of another, and in this way one man can lead a number of horses. I have seen a great string of them tied together in this fashion and when camp was made

THE BOY CAPTIVES

for the night, and the Indians did not want to turn them loose, the lead horse would be brought around and tied to the hindermost horse's tail, and thus form a circle, and they would be allowed to graze that way, around and around.

We were in Arizona, I think, and we crossed a dry desert, and suffered greatly for water. We had to kill colts and drink their blood. This was hard to do, but it was drink blood or starve. When we reached the Isinglass Mountains we found plenty of water and grass in the valleys and snow on the mountain tops. Here we let our horses rest and fatten, while we feasted on red berries, prickly pear apples and sotol heads. We were constantly on the alert, for the American soldiers were trying to annihilate Geronimo and his band in this country, and the Mexican soldiers were on the lookout for him in Mexico. Geronimo, whose Apache name was Goyathlay (one who yawns) was given the name of Geronimo (Jerome), by the Mexicans. He was a Chiricahua Apache, and was born on the headwaters of the Gila river, New Mexico, about 1834. His father was Taklishim (The Gray One), and his mother was known as Juana.

Geronimo was a brave chief, shrewd general, and gave the American and Mexican troops much trouble. There is no telling how many men he killed, and he

THE BOY CAPTIVES

was never touched by a bullet. He wore the black star on his breast, tattooed there as a mark of bravery. He was well known throughout the western country, and his name was one which was calculated to strike terror to the hearts of the settlers.

We went down into New Mexico and met up with a large party of Lipans, and did a lot of trading with them. The Lipans had a trading point somewhere with the Mexicans, and would exchange horses and mules for sugar, coffee, whiskey, tobacco, guns, pistols, beads, red calico and other articles. Geronimo was somewhat suspicious of the Lipans, for he believed the Mexicans were trying to get those Indians to set a snare and capture him for a big reward that had been offered for him and his band, so we did not tarry long with this tribe, but went back to the foot of the Black Hills and joined the Comanches again. The Comanches had just had a big fight with some soldiers and rangers, and had been successful in the battle. Here I found Brother Clint on the battle ground, but at first I hardly recognized him. He had been shot in the side of the head and face, and one eye was badly swollen. He knew me, though, and came to meet me with joy. The chiefs combined their warriors for another attack on the soldiers, but I and Clint and all the boys under fourteen were turned back with the squaws,

THE BOY CAPTIVES

while Geronimo and Tasacowadi and the warriors went to renew the fight. We were moved back about three miles, but we could hear the sounds of the battle as it raged fiercely, until sundown, when they all came to camp. They would not say much about the fight, but indicated that they had them overpowered about three to one. They went back that night and made a charge on the soldier's camp and got some of their horses. I call them soldiers, but they may have been ranchmen and settlers. There were many Indians wounded and some of them died. The Americans left there, and the Indians seemed to be glad the fight was over. From that time on we had a great deal of trouble with the soldiers, rangers and ranchmen, who followed us so persistently that we were kept on the move constantly. We traveled across mountains, on the plains, and over the desert, and when we came near any settlements we made raids and stole horses and killed people. In our ramblings we met up with different tribes of Indians, among them some Yaquis who came out of Mexico. These Yaquis wanted to trade for me and some other white boy captives, but Geronimo would not trade. After they left us it was said the Yaquis were spies sent out from Mexico to learn how large Geronimo's band was. It was not long until a great army of soldiers and rangers were on our trail,

THE BOY CAPTIVES

and we went on towards the Rocky Mountains, where we felt that we would be safe. When we reached there Geronimo and his band went up on a mountain, over a trail so narrow that we ascended with great difficulty. On top of this mountain was a tableland about a mile wide and many miles in length, and in swags we found water which had formed pools during a rainfall. Here we camped, and Geronimo, knowing we were being pursued, placed about 600 warriors to watch the trail up the mountain side. When the soldiers came to the foot of the mountain they camped and did not try to follow us further. They stayed in camp a week or two, waiting for the Indians to come down, but Geronimo was too wise to accommodate them. After the soldiers left we descended the mountain and went further away. And thus we were hounded and kept on the move constantly. We knew the country, though, and where to find the most game, and despite the fact that we were relentlessly pursued by our enemies, we managed to kill game, steal horses, lift scalps, and lead our wild life just the same.

I always found much enjoyment and excitement in killing buffalo, but I will not go into detail and tell of the hunts we participated in, because Brother Clint has already described that.

It was a great sight to see the Indians prepare for a

THE BOY CAPTIVES

big war dance. They would parade all over camp, all painted up, with brass earrings and horn rings, fox caps, with buffalo horns fixed on the caps, and eagle feathers all over them. They would sing war songs, and I remember that at the end of one song they would all crow like a rooster. That meant victory. In hunting wild game the Indians resorted to all kinds of strategies. They would put on deer skins, and antelope skins, and crawl on all fours almost up to any wild animal and kill them. They keep these skins for that purpose.

Geronimo sent a band of about twenty-five warriors over into Arizona, I think it was, to steal some horses, and I was sent along. We rode for several weeks, and came to a settlement where there was considerable irrigation being done, judging from the canals and growing crops. We watched a little ranch for about a half a day, got everything pretty well located, and about an hour before sunset the Indians closed in on the ranch and attacked it. I stayed with the horses, with four or five Indians, a few hundred yards away. When we heard the shooting we went down there and found they had captured the ranch and killed all but two of the people. One girl ran into a cornfield and made her escape. They captured a boy about twelve years old. When we reached there they were scalping

THE BOY CAPTIVES

an old man whom they had killed at the cow-pen. I saw a woman lying dead and scalped at the house. They must have killed a woman inside the house for they had three scalps for me to carry. After ransacking the house they brought the captive boy up to my horse and put him up behind me, and we left there. We traveled until about 2 o'clock that night and camped for a short rest. Early the next morning we resumed our flight, heading northwest. Soon it came a heavy rain storm, with some hail, which delayed us for awhile. Next day we discovered a bunch of men on our trail, and we moved in a gallop for the balance of that day. When the sun went down our pursuers were in sight, so we had to ride on as fast as we could. When darkness came on we traveled some distance further and camped for a few hours of rest. About four o'clock in the morning we started on and when daylight came we were many miles from there, and still going. By noon the sun had dried the ground well and we could travel faster. We halted long enough to kill a horse and roast some of the flesh, the first food we had had in two days and nights. We lost our pursuers and got back to headquarters with the captive and the scalps we had taken. The boy was duly initiated by having his clothing stripped off, and painted by the squaws, and he was given a name, "Pilflentio,"

THE BOY CAPTIVES

which means Cherry Creek. We then moved our camp
again, and after a time came to some Kickapoos, with
whom we camped for awhile. We then went south
and met up with a lot of the Yaqui Indians out of old
Mexico, and we all camped together. They had a lot
of horses and mules which they were taking back to
Mexico, and we decided to go with them. We had a
hard time crossing the Rio Grande river, but we
crossed it and camped with those Yaquis for quite
awhile, and then came back on this side and roamed
around in Arizona. The reader can have no idea of
the various Indian tribes, and the number of members
of each tribe that infested that whole western country
at that time. The hostile range included Mexico, New
Mexico, Colorado, Arizona, Utah, Montana, Nebraska
and western part of Texas. I do not mean to say that
the tribe I was with covered all of this vast expanse of
territory, in this many states, but there were thousands
and thousands of Indians of different tribes, and all
were stealing stock, murdering people and taking children captives. If all of these tribes would have united
against the common foe, the white men, the United
States would probably not have conquered the Indians even to this day.

Did I ever get homesick to return to my people?
You may ask. Of course at first I felt very lonely, but

THE BOY CAPTIVES

I suppose I was too small to worry much about my situation, but at times there would come a longing for the loved ones at home. One day I was sitting in camp gnawing on a horse rib, and was thinking of my home, my brothers and sisters, and of my father, all so far away, and perhaps I would never see them again. And poor Brother Clint, who was in a condition similar to myself, and my grief became unbearable. I laid my bone down and commenced crying. One old squaw came up and asked me why I was crying. I told her an ant had stung me. But it was the sting of loneliness and great sorrow, for I felt that I was without a friend in all the wide world.

We went to the buffalo range, perhaps it was in Kansas or in the Panhandle of Texas, and we killed many of the animals. When buffalo were slaughtered we would have great feasts. The squaws and children would get around and pick off little pieces of the meat and hop around like a bunch of buzzards eating it before it was roasted. While on the buffalo range, I caught a buffalo calf, about a month old, of which had not shed its red hair. It was as red as a Durham calf. When they get older, the red hair gives way to black hair. I killed it with a small pistol and an Indian helped me to butcher it. He took the stomach out and carried it to camp. It was full of milk, which he gave

THE BOY CAPTIVES

to the squaws to drink, and they went after it greedily.

We went down on the line of Old Mexico, and met up with a band of Comanches who had a lot of stolen horses which they intended to take over into Mexico and trade to the Mexicans. We fell in with them and went into Northern Mexico, and met a lot of very friendly Indians. Some of these Indians wore Mexican pants, while others wore only breech-clouts. We all camped together, and a few of these Indians went off from camp one day and were gone several days. When they returned a lot of Mexicans came with them, and brought in a lot of articles to trade, coffee, sugar, whiskey, tobacco, and steel arrow spikes. One of the Mexicans had some dry goods and caps with beads. The trading was brisk. I saw an Indian give a good mule for a cap, and another Indian gave a horse for several yards of red ribbon. But they would not trade for blue and green ribbon, for they said that color would bring them bad luck. A half pound of coffee would easily get a horse, and a horn full of powder would buy a horse, while two large pieces of peloncia (Mexican sugar), would be exchanged for a mule. These traders had some corn meal, but our band would not trade for it. However, the Yaquis bought it and made up a big lot of mush, and we all ate it. One small keg of whiskey would bring two good mules.

THE BOY CAPTIVES

A funny incident occurred here, which I will relate. The Mexicans had an old fashioned piggin full of molasses, and tried to sell it to the Indians, but they were suspicious that it might be poisoned. Finally the trader in order to allay their suspicions, dipped his finger in the molasses and then licked it off. So they all began to dip their fingers in and the licking began. Soon about half of the molasses was gone. An old squaw, after taking a few licks, liked it so well she turned the piggin up and drank the remainder. In a little while the molasses began to boil out of her mouth and nose, and she became deathly sick.

One of the old Yaquis died while we were there and I saw them bury him. They dug a hole and put the body into it, and covered it up with dirt. Then with a big stone they packed the dirt down tight and hard. We soon left these Indians, crossed back into the United States and went up into Colorado, where we found lots of snow and ice in the mountains. I have laid down at night with a rug over me, and next morning I would awake to find about six inches of snow covering me. But I did not get cold. We stayed in those mountains until spring, and then went south, and a party of raiders went out and stole a lot of horses, which they decided to take into Mexico and trade them to the Indians in that country. We went into Arizona,

THE BOY CAPTIVES

and then down about where Bisbee now is located, and crossed into Mexico, and there we met up with some Indians who had just come from Texas. One of the band was a mulatto Negro, who could speak good English. He delighted in tormenting me by saying he had killed my father over in Texas. We stayed around down there a good while, and made several raids upon Mexican settlements, getting a lot of horses which we intended to take back into New Mexico. One day one of the Comanche spies came in and reported that some men were following us, so we moved from there and went north, coming to a long chain of mountains which we could not ascend. Our spies kept close watch on the movements of our pursuers, while we were searching for a pass through those mountains. I stayed behind with the horses and the squaws. Old Chief Geronimo plainly showed his uneasiness, and sent about a hundred warriors back in the rear to protect the camp followers. Finally the Mexican soldiers overtook us about 2 o'clock one afternoon, and the fight opened up. We could not do anything with the loose horses we were driving and as they could not run far on account of being in a canyon we abandoned them. The battle which was fought there was a desperate one and continued about three hours, the Mexicans pouring a deadly fire into our band. The soldiers kept com-

THE BOY CAPTIVES

ing closer, and I tried to run, but my horse fell down and I fell off with my gun in hand. I waited a moment or two for my horse to get up, but he still lay there, and I sought a safe place in which to hide. I found a little cave and went into it, but it did not extend very far back, so I turned around on my hands and knees and looked out. I could see my chief, Geronimo, hanging on the side of his horse, with one arm around under the horse's neck, and making arrows fly. And I'll wager he emptied several saddles that day. That was the last time I saw Geronimo until I saw him in San Antonio several years afterward, when he was a captive.

The Mexicans were victorious in this fight, and the Indians took to the hills, while I was in the cave, holding it down. When the Indians left the Mexicans began to search for whatever they could find, picking up guns, arrows, and killing the wounded. They were about ready to leave when one Mexican climbed up to where I was concealed and looked into the cave and saw me. He called to others to come, and soon a lot of them were there motioning for me to come out. I left my gun in the cave and came crawling out, and held up my hands in token of surrender. They searched me, and then reached into the little cave and brought forth my gun.

THE BOY CAPTIVES

So there I was, still a captive, but in the hands of the Mexicans. I did not know what they would do with me, but I thought they would treat me as the Indians had done, and naturally I was indifferent. They took me to their nearest town, and probably having heard that my father had offered $1,000 reward for me, they kept me closely guarded until they could get word to the authorities at San Antonio. In due time the money was sent to Mexico City, and then I was taken to San Antonio to be delivered to the sheriff there, and later restored to my people. When we reached San Antonio father's nearest neighbor, Mr. Aue, who owned the store and was postmaster at Leon Springs, learned that I had arrived, and as he was well acquainted with the sheriff, he persuaded him to allow me to go home with him. He put me in his buggy and took me out to his ranch, a distance of about twenty miles. I did not know what was coming next. The wild life I had led the past few years had made me afraid of white people, and I had fears that I had been sold to this man by the Mexicans, not knowing I was going home to my own father. I wondered if he would tie me to a tree and put another brand upon me. But he treated me very kindly that night and locked me in a room where there was a nice clean bed. But I did not sleep in it. I preferred laying down

THE BOY CAPTIVES

Geronimo
Chief of the notorious Band
Of Apache Indians
photo by Ed Irwin 1897

THE BOY CAPTIVES

upon the floor, for that, to me, was more comfortable. Next morning I was given a good breakfast, and then my guardian put me in his buggy again and we started for somewhere else. He would talk to me, but I did not know what he was saying. I had forgotten my native tongue, so I would only grunt and point down the road. It was about eight miles to my father's place, and as we drew nearer I began to recognize different places that were familiar to me. I should have stated above that I had been given clean clothing and my long hair had been cut off, and I was not painted up.

When we reached father's place he came out to greet his friend, and invited him to get out and come in. I followed behind them, and when they sat down on the porch Father gave me a chair. I did not know what was coming next, so I sat very still, and wondered. Just then I saw my brother Clinton, slipping around the corner of the fence. He would peep over and take a look at me, and then dodge back again. I knew him, but I was afraid to make a movement. Papa and Mr. Aue talked for some time, and Mr. Aue was waiting to see if Father would recognize me. Finally dinner was announced, and Mr. Aue said to Father, "This little boy has been with the Indians a long time, and maybe he can tell you something about your boy." Papa stopped and looked at me very

THE BOY CAPTIVES

straight, and then recognized me. He grabbed me into his arms and began to hug me. Then here came the balance of the family to greet me, and all was excitement. Clint knew me all the time, but was afraid to say anything. There was great joy in that home that day, and Father was almost beside himself. He would walk the floor and say it was God's blessing that had restored his two boys to him.

There is not much more to tell. We two boys were pretty wild at first, and had no manners of any kind except those which we had learned from the Indians, and that did not fit very well in polite society. But we were happy in each other's company and our family bestowed every kindness and sympathy upon us, until the gentle refining influences of home life began to have its effect and we became civilized again. At first we were always into some sort of devilment, on one occasion taking father's gun out and killed a neighbor's cow and was roasting the beef when we were found by our brother-in-law, Jack Cravey.

Old Geronimo and his band kept up their raids, until General Miles and his soldiers, in August, 1886, captured him and his band, numbering 340. Geronimo was first taken to Florida, later to Alabama, and finally to Fort Sill, Oklahoma, where he was kept until his death which occurred a few years ago. When he

THE BOY CAPTIVES

was captured he was brought through San Antonio under guard, and I went to see him there. The old fellow recognized me instantly, and called my by my name, and I had a long talk with him. I met other members of the tribe at the same time, and they all wanted me to get the white people to release them and they would promise to be good. As I started to leave them they would catch me around the neck and beg me to stay with them. I told them I would come back again.

MY COWBOY EXPERIENCE

When I, Clinton L. Smith, was brought back from captivity, and was restored to my father, I remained with him for some time, herding sheep, and doing such work on the ranch as was given to me to do, but I was not satisfied. My brother-in-law, Leonard Coker gave me a small mare, and I soon broke her to the saddle and found her a splendid animal. I made up my mind to run away. By this time I had become reconciled to the ways of white people, and did not want to return to the Indians. I had heard of the trail, and had considerable experience with cattle, and I decided to go to some ranch in West Texas, get me a job as cowpuncher, and go up the trail. I was then about seventeen years old, and strong and husky. One night I

THE BOY CAPTIVES

saddled my little mare and pulled out. I had no money, but that made no difference to me, for I was on my way, and cared not where I was going. Next morning I came to a Mexican camp and got breakfast there. I passed several ranches and asked for work, but was turned down. That night I stopped at a ranch and they treated me very kindly. The next morning I offered the ranchmen my coat in payment for my night's lodging, but he would not take it. He told me about a big cow camp on the Nueces river, about forty miles below Uvalde, where cattle were being gathered for a drive up the trail in the spring. This was in February. I went to this camp, reaching there about sundown one evening. When I rode up and asked for work the boss told me to get down and stay all night. He told me they were catching wild cattle out of the brush, and had to rope all of them, and while he could not use my services I was welcome to stay there awhile and let my pony rest. Next day I helped the cook get wood and water, and assisted the horse wrangler with the horses, he having about thirty to attend to. One morning when the horses were in an old brush pen the wrangler had considerable trouble roping them, and when he missed a throw the horse would jump out of the pen and get away. I asked him to let me try to rope one, and he gave me the rope. And every time I

THE BOY CAPTIVES

threw that rope I caught a horse. This seemed to surprise the boss and he asked me where I learned to rope so well. I told him "on a sheep ranch." He said that as I could handle a rope so well I could help them catch wild cattle out of the brush, and gave me one of his saddle horses to use. These cattle were so wild they would come out of the brush only at night to graze along the open places and flats along the river, and the cowboys would work by moonlight. The brush, which was catclaw, mesquite, black brush and prickly pear, was so thick they could not ride through it in daytime, so they would lay in wait at night and catch these cattle when they came to water and to graze. When a wild steer was roped he would be necked to a tree until next day when the catch would be taken to a pasture and held while others were being caught. The boss' name was Pete Cline, and he offered to pay me $25 per month, which I was only too glad to accept. We worked there for some time and caught quite a number of the wild cattle. In the remuda was an outlaw horse, grey in color with zebra stripes on his legs, and no one could ride him. I told some of the boys if they would saddle old Outlaw for me I would ride him. The cook tried to persuade me not to attempt the feat, but I had ridden worse horses than old Outlaw, while I was with the Indians, and I was

THE BOY CAPTIVES

not afraid. I put on my spurs, put a blindfold on him, fixed the hackamore good, and mounted him. He stood perfectly still, until I raised the blinds and caught him with my big spurs. He went straight up and when he came down he came bawling like a calf. That horse did everything but talk Mexican to me. He pitched all over the landscape, until he gave out, but I stayed with him, and when I dismounted he was completely conquered. The boss was so pleased that he gave him to me to ride for a long time. The boss asked me many questions about where and how I learned to ride so well, but I answered evasively. I did not tell him I had spent several years with the Indians; in fact I did not want it to be known that I had run away from home, for I was afraid I would be discharged and sent back to my father.

We gathered the herd and prepared to start on the trail. The road brand was a circle around the hip bone, and was easy to make. The boss told me I could go along, at $30 a month, and help Lazarene, the Mexican horse wrangler, with these horses, there being about sixty-five head in the remuda, and many of them wild. My old saddle, being no good, was discarded and the boss bought me a new one, paying $26 for it. Now good saddles sell for $75 to $100. On the 10th day of March, 1875, the great herd was rounded up

THE BOY CAPTIVES

and thrown over on the Nueces river to be counted. The herd numbered about four thousand old Texas longhorns, the ages ranging from four to twelve years, all colors, some spotted, black, yellow, blue, roan, brindle, with horns three feet long and as wild as they could be. When all was in readiness we started on the long drive to Nebraska. The fourth night we camped about five miles above Uvalde, near a little mountain. That night the cattle stampeded, but the boys stayed with them, and when morning came most of the herd was in Uvalde. We had to remain here for a day while the boys hunted for missing steers. Lazarene and I had all of the horses together. We drifted on up the river; grass was fine. When we reached Barksdale, at which time there was only one little box store there, the cattle were divided into three bunches on account of the driving through that rough country. We went out on the Divide, where Rocksprings is now located, and camped for the night. About 10 o'clock the boss called all hands out to help with the cattle, for a great storm was coming up from the northwest. The storm struck us about 2 o'clock a.m., and we had great difficulty in holding the cattle. But we milled them around and around, and the boys would sing to them, and we held them until daylight, when part of the boys went to camp to get breakfast and change horses, and

THE BOY CAPTIVES

when they returned those remaining on herd went in. We counted our herd and found about 300 missing, so the boss sent me and some of the other boys back to look for them. We found all but forty head, and Lans Deats and myself went further on back to continue the search while the other boys drove the recovered bunch to the herd. When we found the cattle they were mixed up with other wild cattle, and we had a hard time getting them back, taking the other wild cattle with them. When we got back to the herd we began cutting out the strays, when the boss rode up and said, "Let them stay in the herd and we will have some beer money." We road branded them and from there on we picked up lots of those beer-money cattle. From there on Pete Cline put me with the cattle and put another boy in my place with the remuda.

We cut across the country to the Llano draws, and from there to the San Saba, then to the Kickapoo, and camped on the Lipan Flat one night. It was then called Buckhorn Flat, I think. After supper a dark, threatening cloud came up, and we had to ride herd all night, talking and singing to those wild steers to keep them quiet. About daylight a horse shook himself, and that scared the cattle, and away they went pell mell, and we had to ride hard to throw them into a mill, and soon they quieted down, and just as the sun rose they

THE BOY CAPTIVES

were quietly grazing as if nothing had happened to excite them. When we reached the Concho river it was on a small rise, but we crossed the herd without trouble and went ten miles further, threw the herd off the trail, and camped. The trail was well beaten out from so many herds passing north. Every morning we would let the cattle graze off the trail and when they were full we would drive them back to the trail, and they would string out and march along for several miles; then they would want to graze again, and were allowed to do so for about two miles. We usually made seven miles in the morning and seven miles in the afternoon. The cook and the remuda would go on ahead of the herd, and have dinner ready when we got there at noon. We changed horses only at night. Our night horses were the best ones we had.

When we reached Cow Gap the weather was fine, and everything was lovely. Next we came to a region I at once recognized, for I had been there while I was with the Indians. The Cross L ranch was located there. The owner of that ranch came to our camp one night and had a sociable chat with our boss. He asked where we were from and when the boss told him, he said he knew of an old man living down in the country who had two boys stolen by the Indians, and when he got them back one of them ran off and was not heard of

THE BOY CAPTIVES

again. That was getting pretty close to me, but I kept my mouth shut.

We crossed the Colorado and went by Coleman City, which at that time had only a few houses. Our herd had to swim the Colorado, and our chuck wagon was rafted across. After crossing this river, one day at noon Bill Brady was sitting on his rope while eating dinner and his horse got scared and made a run on the rope, which became entangled in Bill's spurs and he was dragged for quite a distance. He was laid up for several days, and was carried along in the chuck wagon. We went on to the Brazos, and then to the Red River, crossing into the Indian Territory. One day a trail cutter named Jack Rose came to our herd and held us up for a whole day looking through it for other people's cattle, but he did not find any. A big bunch of Indians came to us one day and wanted Cline to give them some beeves. He cut out five or six big stags and they drove them out to one side and butchered them. One of the Indians rode up and called me by my Indian name, and I shook my head. I did not want Pete Cline or any of the cowboys to know that I had lived with the Indians. We crossed Sweetwater, and could see the Wichita Mountains in the distance, and I felt like I was back home with the Indians again. We had a long dry drive before we got to Dodge City,

THE BOY CAPTIVES

Kansas, on the Arkansas River, arriving there about the 19th of June. From Dodge City, we headed for Longhorn, Nebraska, crossing the Smoky River, and other big streams which were swimming from heavy rains. We went out of Kansas into Nebraska and struck the Platte River, taking up that stream to Longhorn, where we were met by the owners of the herd, Mr. Goodman of Comal county, and Mr. Flowers of Uvalde. This was about the latter part of August. The cattle and horses were sold there, and the hands went from camp to town in a big ambulance wagon, and from there, next day, went further back to a new tap road where we took the train for Texas. I came back as far as Fort Worth with Pete Cline, and then on the stage to San Antonio, reaching there about the 15th of September, and went out to the ranch with Mr. Cline, and broke horses for him.

The next spring Flowers, John Lytle and some other men began to gather a big herd to drive north. Lytle bought about 800 down near Oakville, and we went after them, and brought them up to San Antonio where he received about 600 more. The road brand was LD. We loaded our supplies at Oppenheimer's store, and started the herd up the Helotes road, going by the old Gallagher ranch where we received about a thousand more big steers, and headed for Bandera. We camped

THE BOY CAPTIVES

the first night from there on the Newcomer Flat on Pipe Creek. We went through Bandera Pass to Kerrville. This was in March, 1876. From Kerrville we went on to Noxville, where we received some more cattle from Rufe Light, and branded them at the old Creed Taylor ranch. We drove this herd through to Chug Hole, Wyoming, and had a long hard trip of it, with stampedes, thunder storms, high water, Indians and the usual trimmings to contend with. We reached our destination September 7th, where the cattle were turned over to the buyer and turned loose on the range. I came back to Austin on the train and from Austin to San Antonio, where I bought a horse and went to see my sister, Mrs. Coker, nine miles out. From there I went home to see my father, having been absent two years. He was very glad to see me, and treated me affectionately. I remained with him two years, helping with the farm and ranch work, and in 1878 I went back to cow driving, getting a job with Bill Blocker, who started 1600 two and three year olds up the trail. We went to the left of San Antonio, out to the Leon, and road branded with a B high upon the back. Went on to the Haby settlement on the Medina river, and received 600 more from the Habys. Later Buck Hamilton turned in about 400. Buck was sheriff of Bandera county at that time. Mr. Devine was our boss

THE BOY CAPTIVES

when we started out, but was replaced by Sam Johnson, an old trail cutter. Near Coolidge, Kansas, our cook was shot and killed by a boy named McGee. At Trail City, Colorado, a cowboy named Bluford and I quit the herd, and went to work on ranches.

We heard of a big fair at Pueblo, Colorado, where they were to stage a roping and riding event, so we went up there and entered the contest. There were eighteen entries, and four prizes. The first prize was $125; second $75; third $50; and fourth $25. The entrance fee was $25; I won first prize, and when the contest was over the winners were lined up and their photograph was taken, and each winner was numbered, as follows: C. L. Smith, first; Bedy Hamilton, second; L. Riles, third; Charlie Hammonds, fourth. That was forty-eight years ago, and I still have that photograph, which I treasure most highly. I have roped a good many times in contests, but usually won second prize.

Bluford and I went to New Mexico, near Silver City, to join the rangers. Harve Whitehall was sheriff of Grant county, New Mexico, at that time, and Lew Wallace was governor of the territory. J. W. Flemming had organized a company to drive back the Indians, and I was employed by him as a spy and trailer, near Silver City. We were engaged in this work for some

THE BOY CAPTIVES

time, and had several fights with renegades. Later we resigned and went to work on a ranch that employed about sixty men, and claims to run 10,000 cattle and a thousand horses. While working on this ranch I helped in the biggest roundup I ever saw take place. We broke horses there for some time receiving $5 to $7 per head for breaking. While I was there I went with a lot of the ranch hands down into Old Mexico and found a good many stolen cattle and horses belonging to the ranch among the Yaqui Indians. We rounded up all we could find, about 300 head, and brought them back into New Mexico. If the Mexican authorities had found us there we would have had some trouble. We returned to Texas the following November. I went home and helped my father that winter, but when spring came I was like a wild goose and wanted to go north.

I went down to the King ranch and broke horses, and Mr. King employed me to take a bunch of 1200 horses up the trail. My hands were all Mexicans. I sold horses all along the trail, and when they were all sold I returned to the King ranch with the Mexican hands. Mr. King wanted me to take a herd up the trail the next spring, but I did not want to go. Lee Jones and I went to work on the Tinning ranch on the San Geronimo, 27 miles from San Antonio, where we

THE BOY CAPTIVES

broke wild horses and branded colts. We worked here six months and rode many old outlaw horses. Some kind of wild animals were killing Mr. Tinning's colts, and one day Bart Welch and I went out into the Gallagher Mountains with a pack of hounds to run the varmints down. The hounds soon found the trail which led off in the direction of the Medina River, and after a run of about five miles the dogs bayed at the mouth of a cave. We tried to make the dogs go in there, but they would not go, so I crawled into the cave to punch it out. I gave Bart my pistol to hold, and when I crawled away back in the cave it was so dark in there I could not see anything. I pulled off my shirt, rolled it up and made a torch of it. Not seeing anything in the cave I turned around to go out and as I did so I saw two balls of fire. They were the eyes of a Mexican lion which had hidden in a pocket of the cave and allowed me to pass him. I was in a close place, but I began to crawl toward the animal with my torch, and it began to growl and back out. When he got to the opening Bart Welch shot him and the dogs tackled him, and soon he was our meat. We skinned the big animal and took the pelt to San Antonio and sold it to Ed Van Riper. Bart Welch and Lee Jones are living yet.

Brother Jeff and I worked for a long time for Willie

THE BOY CAPTIVES

Capps out on Dry Salado Creek, ten miles north of San Antonio. Capps, Brother Jeff and I made up a herd of horses to take up the trail; Capps had 500 head and Jeff and I had 160 head. Dug Nail had about forty head which he put into the herd, making about 700 altogether, and in April, 1884, we started. Our outfit consisted of Dug Nail, Jim Coker, Jeff Smith, C. L. Smith, Wiley Capps, Jim Brady, Buffalo Bob and Willie Maltsberger. Ben Cravey and Jim Tomerlin helped us start. At Doan's store on Red River one of our colts gave out and we sent Brother Jeff to the store to see if he could trade it for anything. Mr. Doan asked him how much he wanted for the colt and Jeff told him he thought ten dollars would be about right. Doan said he would take the colt if Jeff would take the amount in trade, so Jeff came back to camp with ten dollars worth of red handkerchiefs and candy. When we reached Dodge City, Kansas, we had sold all of the horses except about eighty head. The boys came home on the train, while I drove the remnant of the herd to Trail City, Colorado, and sold fifty saddle horses at $50 a round. The remainder were wild horses, and I threw them into a herd bound for Nebraska, and accepted a job with the outfit at $40 a month. When I sold all of the horses I returned to Texas, and this was my last trip up the trail.

I worked for Nat Lewis on the Leon, and for other

THE BOY CAPTIVES

well known ranchmen of that section of Texas. I went on several trips with Charley Cravey to Chicago with trainloads of cattle. I also worked for Monroe Saner of Boerne, and bought cattle for Captain Charles Schreiner of Kerrville, putting the Y brand on them and delivering them at the big pens on Goat Creek.

I could relate many interesting experiences connected with my life as a cowboy and ranch hand, but space forbids. My story must draw to its close.

On August 29th, 1889 I was happily married to Miss Dixie Alamo Dyche, at the Gilliam ranch on the Medina River. Mr. Gilliam gave us a big wedding feast, and helped to set us up in housekeeping. I bought cattle for him and looked after his ranch for a long time. Eugene Leibold lived with us and Billie Riggs helped us also. Claud Gilliam married Miss Riggs, and Thad Gilliam married Miss Ida Pennington. I accumulated a bunch of cattle and moved them up to Sterling county and lost some of them that winter. The balance I sold to a Mr. Tankersley and returned to the Gilliam ranch. Later I bought a little ranch at Pipe Creek, Bandera county, and while running a steer one day my horse fell with me and I sustained a broken leg and I was laid up for a long time. Afterwards I sold my Pipe Creek ranch and bought another one on Hicks Creek; Ben Farris owns it now.

In 1910 I bought a ranch in Edwards county, and I am living on it today.

CLINTON LAFAYETTE SMITH
1859-1932

Clinton (Clint) Lafayette Smith, son of Henry M. and Fanny (Short) Smith, was born in Kendall County, Texas. Clint, age 11, and his brother Jeff, age 9, were kidnapped by Lipan and Comanche Indians while herding sheep near their home in 1871. Clint was adopted by Chief Tasacowadi and lived with the Comanche for five years, until he gave himself up in a trade for Indians imprisoned at Fort Sill, Oklahoma. After returning to his family, Smith became a trail driver and Angora goat breeder. He moved to Rocksprings in 1910 with his wife, Dixie (Dyche) and children.

Recorded by Texas Historical Commission in 2001

JEFFERSON DAVIS SMITH
1862-1940

Jefferson (Jeff) Davis Smith, son of Henry M. and Fanny (Short) Smith, was born in Kendall County, Texas. Jeff, age 9, and his brother Clint, age 11, were kidnapped by Lipan and Comanche Indians while herding sheep near their home in 1871. Jeff was reportedly bought by Apache Chief Geronimo and made to join his tribe. Mexican bandits captured him to return him to his family for a $1000 reward about 1878. He married Julia Harriet Reed in 1894 and moved to San Antonio.

Recorded by Texas Historical Commission in 1993

Copy

Comal Co. October 1st, '71.

To the Hon Mr Belknap;
Secretary of War.

Sir

I wish to inform you that I have not yet obtained my lost children, also that Mr Tatum has informed me that there is a boy in the hands of the Comanches whom he believes to be mine; he has applied to Col. Grierson of Fort Sill, also to Col. McKenzie of Fort Richardson to recover the captive held by Moaway's band of Comanches. Now, my dear Sir, can you not issue an order to those officers that will be effective for their recovery; if one child is there, both doubtless are. It is hard, Sir, to think that my poor, little boys are held in wretched captivity by those rascals, & the U.S. troops right at their doors; & the villain, Moaway, even had the audacity to tell Mr Tatum to his face that 'he did not know whether his men would give up the boy or not? Now, my dear Sir, I beg, aye, pray you to use the power you possess to effect the recovery of my poor suffering boys. Mr. Tatum has done all he has the power to do, without success; he has no power to force them, & this is what they need.

Hoping, Sir, that you will attend to this important matter, I remain,

Your obed servant.

(Signed) H. M. Smith.

P.S. My P.O. is Boerne, Kendall Co Texas.

Piedras Negras, Mexico
April 7th 1873

Editor San Antonio Express

Sir; By a Mexican trader I have received information that the Lipan Indians now in Camps with the Muscaleros and Comanches at the mouth of the canon of San Rodrigo, have in their possession a white boy from 8 to 9 years old, whom they captured in Texas, 2 years ago.

According to the statement of the said trader the boys parents must live on the Cibolo & there own large flocks of sheep, the boy was looking after some shepherds in his fathers employ at the time he was captured.

I have commissioned the said Trader to ransom the boy, in which he expects to succeed by paying one hundred dollars more or less for him. In about 20 days from now I expect to hear of the result of the mans mission.

Letters to me can be directed via Eagle Pass.

Very respectfully
Wm Schuchard
U.S. Commercial Agent

Eagle Pass Texas
May 1st 1873

Bvt Myr Gnl C C Auger
Cmdg. Dept of Texas
San Antonio Texas
General

Today I succeeded
in getting Mr H M Smith's son, who
was captured (from near Boerne) by the
Indians some two years ago.
The boy, Jeff, goes down on the stage
tomorrow morning, consigned to the
Stage Agent at San Antonio, Mr Muncey.

We hope to start into Mexico, on
our mission as soon as the necessary
arrangements can be completed.

very respectfully
yours
Thos G Williams
Special Indian Agent &c

Copy.
Asgo, Lit Society, 71.
3598 AG.O. 1871.
17 G.I.H. I. 1871.
Comal Co., Texas.
Oct. 1, 1871.

H. M. Smith.
Asks military
assistance in re-
covering his children,
held by Comanche
Indians.

Ref? from War Dept.

Copies to Gen? Grierson
& Gen? MacKenzie—
..../500
2342 & 2120 A.G. 71
File Fizewith
Sill
L.S. 1469. D.J. 1871.

Rec L.S. No. — S. 1871
P Ag. O., Oct. 18. 1871.

1st Endorsement.

Adjutant General's Office
Washington, Oct. 24, 1871.

Official copy
respectfully referred
— through Headquarters
Military Division of the
South — to the Command-
ing Officer Department
of Texas, for report.
By order:

E D Townsend
Adjutant General.
54. 7
276.

Second Indorsement.
Hdqrs Mily Div. South
Louisville Ky. Oct. 28. 1871.
Respectfully transmitted
to the Comdg Officer Dept Texas.
By order Maj. Gen Halleck
Wm Power
Capt. 3rd arty. A.D.C
A. A. A. General,